Praise for *Meant To Be*

"Walter Anderson's eloquent and beautiful memoir is an offering: I have rarely read in recent years a narrative written with such intensity, emotion, and elegance. I warmly recommend it to all readers, whatever their faith."

—Elie Wiesel

"The magic of this memoir is that we are able to take the journey with Walter, so raw and revealing, right to the day he discloses the secret he held inside for thirty-four years. As we read, we learn something about our own lives that is priceless. I highly recommend this book." —Dr. Joyce Brothers

"Part mystery, part Horatio Alger story, Walter Anderson's uplifting memoir takes us on one man's journey from troubled youth to noble citizen, as he unlocks the startling secret of his childhood and discovers the kind of spiritual enlightenment we all seek. Anderson keeps us rooting for him from start to finish, all the while reminding us that the real key to life is in never losing our capacity to love. This book moved me to tears." —Marlo Thomas

"Walter Anderson has written a marvelous book that will linger in our memory. Only a man truly at peace with himself could write with such rigorous honesty about the love he received from his mother and the anger he felt for his father. Amid the complexity born in violence, he manages to find a clarity that affirms life. Not an easy task—but this beautifully written book pulls it off."

—Bill Bradley

"I stayed up all night reading. . . . A great story beautifully told by a great storyteller." —Edward Klein

"This riveting story will hold the reader's attention from beginning to end (Warning to reader: Keep a box of tissues nearby). Anyone who wants not only to achieve success in their own life but to positively impact the lives of others will be inspired. Many thanks to Walter Anderson for exposing his life and making himself vulnerable in order to give others encouragement and hope."

—Benjamin S. Carson, Sr., M.D.,
Professor and Director of Pediatric Neurosurgery,
Johns Hopkins Medical Institutions

"Anderson . . . relates his up-by-the-bootstraps success story with humility and awe. As he reveals his life through illustrative anecdotes that take him from the jungles of Vietnam to audiences with heads of state, Anderson's abiding spirituality, compassion, and appreciation for the essence of family are confirmed within the context of one courageous man's pursuit of the American dream."

—*Booklist*

"What begins as the wrenching recollection of a 1950s teen from a tenement near the Bronx evolves unexpectedly into a disarming meditation on family ties and the power of the pen. Who could have envisioned this high school dropout becoming pals with Nobel Laureate Elie Wiesel? Or that a shocking revelation about his abusive father would at once shatter and shape Anderson's identity, beliefs, and vocation? In his journey from pint-size pool shark to *Parade* magazine editor, there are many milestones worth mentioning. But one will stick with me: 'Just What Is Vietnam?', the letter soon-to-be Sergeant Anderson wrote for himself and his fellow Marines. It was his first published piece, and in it you'll find just why he was meant to be a writer."

—*Entertainment Weekly* (A-)

"As the CEO of Parade Publications, Walter Anderson knows how to tell a good story. Now he's written his own personal drama, the deeply felt *Meant To Be*."
—*Reader's Digest* (Editor's Choice/Featured Selection)

"An engaging, inspiring book."   —*Houston Chronicle*

"An inspiring memoir. *Meant To Be* raises interesting questions about what it means to be Jewish and the role of heredity in the development of a human being."   —*Jewish Book World*

"A lean, readable, and sanguine memoir celebrating an adult rite of passage."
—*Kirkus Reviews*

"An engrossing story. Anderson does an exceptional job of illuminating how powerful belief in oneself can be and the beauty of possibility in the face of despair and uncertainty."   —*St. Petersburg Times*

About the Author

WALTER ANDERSON is chairman and CEO of Parade Publications and an advisory board member of Literacy Volunteers of America and the National Center for Family Literacy. A high school dropout, he is a national spokesperson for GED and director of the National Dropout Prevention Fund. Additionally, he is a member of the board of advisors of the U.S. Naval Postgraduate School and the National Council on Economic Education. Anderson is also the creator of a series of filmed discussions with prominent Americans called "It's About Time" and was the 1994 recipient of the Horatio Alger Award. He has appeared on such television programs as *Today, CBS Nightwatch,* and the *Sally Jessy Raphael Show.* He lives in White Plains, New York, with his wife.

ALSO BY WALTER ANDERSON

Courage Is a Three-Letter Word
The Greatest Risk of All
Read with Me
The Confidence Course

Meant
To Be

*The True Story of a Son Who
Discovers He Is His Mother's Deepest Secret*

WALTER ANDERSON

Perennial

An Imprint of HarperCollinsPublishers

First Perennial edition published 2004.

DESIGNED BY SARAH MAYA GUBKIN

The Library of Congress has catalogued the hardcover edition as follows:

Anderson, Walter.
    Meant to be / Walter Anderson.—1st ed.
      p. cm.
    ISBN 0-06-009906-2
     1. Anderson, Walter. 2. Problem families—United States. 3. Secrecy—
    Psychological aspects. 4. Publishers and publishing—United States—Biography.
    I. Title.

    CT275.A715A3 2003
    973.92'092--dc21
    [B]

                                                                2003041661

ISBN 0-06-009907-0 (pbk.)

04 05 06 07 08 ❖/RRD 10 9 8 7 6 5 4 3 2 1

For Si Newhouse, who has so encouraged me past and present,
and to my grandson Jonathan and his cousin Andrew,
who will both live the future of this story.

Meant
To Be

CHAPTER 1

I IMMEDIATELY RECOGNIZED the blue suit. He had bought it years before from Mr. Freeman, a salesman who sold clothes and shoes door-to-door in our old neighborhood. This suit—the only one he owned—had seen some weddings and retirement dinners in its time, but mainly it had been worn to funerals. And now it had arrived at its last funeral: his.

The morticians had carefully dressed him in the old blue suit, a white shirt and a blue tie, then placed his body inside a polished wood casket, arranging his forearms so that his right hand crossed neatly over his left. It was on his face, though, where the craftsmen of the Burr Davis Funeral Home in Mount Vernon, New York, had proved their craft, accomplishing a remarkable feat: The late William Henry Anderson seemed serene—his eyes closed, his expression neutral, as if he were enjoying a deep and peaceful sleep.

Where is the rage now? I wondered.

A few hours earlier, my brother Bill had given me a copy of the obituary that had appeared that day, February 7, 1966, in the local newspaper, the *Daily Argus*:

William H. (Whitey) Anderson Sr., 56, a retired troubleshooter for Con Edison, died yesterday at the U.S. Veterans Hospital in the Bronx.

Mr. Anderson, son of the late Henry W. and Edith (Heikkela) Anderson, was born April 23, 1909, in New Rochelle. A Mount Vernon resident for 35 years, he was a volunteer fireman in Engine 2 and company captain for 14 years. He was a World War II veteran.

Surviving are his wife, Ethel (Crolly) Anderson; two sons, William H. Anderson Jr. of Mount Vernon and Sgt. Walter H. Anderson, a U.S. Marine; a daughter, Mrs. Carol Gennimi of Yorktown Heights; a sister, Mrs. Dhyne Seacord of Elmhurst, L.I.; and five grandchildren.

I remembered his boast: "When I go, they'll all be there!" And they were. The funeral parlor was filled. Dozens of firemen who knew him from his days as a volunteer filled the rear rows. Former co-workers from Con Edison, relatives and family friends from Mount Vernon, Saratoga, New Jersey and Long Island had found seats or queued in the side aisles.

My sister, Carol, was seated in the front row next to my mother. My brother, who had been an Engine 2 volunteer himself but was now a paid firefighter, finished greeting his fellow firemen, then joined me standing in the rear.

"I don't see any of the Cheatham brothers," I told Bill. "Aren't they coming?"

From the age of five until I quit high school at sixteen to enlist in the Marines, we had lived in a tenement on the corner of Eleventh Avenue and Third Street—directly across from Cheatham Brothers Moving and Storage Company.

"No," Bill said. "The Cheathams won't be coming. Out of respect. Mom told me they called her."

Strange, I thought, that my brother didn't say the words "colored" or "Negro" or "black." He knew that his father's best friends, his favorite drinking buddies, were absent because of their race, that they must have decided their presence would cause discomfort or be unwelcome.

I guess I was still mulling this contradiction after the eulogy began, because the minister was well into it before I realized that I didn't recognize the man whose virtues he was praising: "Loved and loving"? How about "feared"? "Kind"? How about "rough"? "Respect for the Scriptures"? Where did that come from?

"Who the hell is he talking about?" my brother whispered. "The old man would not go for this."

"Amen," I said.

Then my mother—to the genuine surprise of my brother, my sister, me and probably everyone else in the room who knew her well—began crying hysterically, pleading, "Willie, take me with you!" Before we left the parlor, my sister, brother and I did our best to soothe her, and we must have succeeded, because she was relaxed when we got her home.

Two days later, the pastor spoke only briefly at the Beechwoods Cemetery in New Rochelle. My sister, her husband and I then drove to my mother's one-bedroom apartment in Mount Vernon, where I was staying on emergency leave from the Marines.

"When are you going back to San Diego?" my sister asked me.

"I have to return to the base by Saturday," I told her. "Meanwhile, I'll stay with Mommy, so she won't be alone."

"Now that Daddy is gone, are you still planning to stay in California when you're discharged?"

I knew that really wasn't meant to be a question. Carol was persistent.

Now that I had returned safely from Vietnam, my sister wanted her little brother to come home forever.

"California's my future," I said, and in an attempt to quickly close the discussion, I added, "I'm going to go to college there."

"They have colleges here, you know," Carol persisted.

"Thanks," I said. "I knew that."

She made a face. This was merely the second or third round of Carol's campaign, I was sure. I could count on more discussions over the next couple of days before I returned to San Diego.

About an hour later, after my sister and her husband had gone, my mother and I sat alone in her living room. As we spoke, I could see her demeanor change dramatically. She was at ease now, talkative, even lively.

I encouraged her as she reminisced, and I listened closely as she again repeated in detail the circumstances surrounding her husband's death, which had been caused by a cerebral hemorrhage. She described the funeral, who had come, what they had said. She recalled for me the best times of her marriage, then the worst. It was as if she had an overpowering need to express herself. It was a bursting dam. Finally the flood subsided, and she sat quietly.

"Mom," I said, "I have one question."

"What, honey?"

"The man we just buried . . ."

"Yes?"

"Was he my father?"

CHAPTER 2

I HAD BEEN DEEP IN SLEEP in the middle of the night when the first slap shocked me awake. I instinctively cringed, covering my face with my hands, drawing my body away from the blows. I smelled whiskey. Wavering before me was my father, his face red, his eyes narrowed in rage, his fists clenched high to strike me again, his voice bellowing, "You can't fool me! You think I was born yesterday? I know what you're going to do . . ."

He struck my arms away as if they were paper. "And I'll make sure you don't!" His voice became even louder. "I'll beat you until I get the truth!"

Although I was just twelve years old, I knew not to cry out, not to protest that I was being beaten for something I *might* do, some accusation I could not defend myself against, some transgression boiling in my father's mind at two o'clock in the morning.

As he lifted his right fist higher, I drew my knees to my chest and, in a futile gesture, tried to tuck in my face. He drove his hands through my knees, grabbed my undershirt and the flesh of my chest, squeezed and started to lift me when my mother burst into the room shouting, "You leave that boy alone!"

My father dropped me back on the bed, ready to turn his rage on his wife. With one hand, she seemed to be trying to wipe her eyes awake while, with the other, she clutched her cotton bathrobe tightly closed.

"What do you think *you're* going to do?" he demanded, his voice hoarse and challenging. He glared at my mother, who was barely five feet three. His eyes blinked slowly, and his body—as thick and muscular as a professional wrestler's, at five feet ten and nearly two hundred pounds—weaved slightly from side to side.

"Well, what are you . . . ?" he started, his words coming slowly and slurred.

"Now, honey," my mother interrupted, her voice soft and gentle.

"I don't care about you either," he told her, his voice not as loud but still belligerent. "You don't mean nothing to me."

Her voice stayed gentle, and she coaxed him as you would a puppy: "Come on, honey, let's go to the kitchen so I can make you something to eat."

"I'm not hungry," he argued.

"Sure you are," she said softly, moving herself between him and my bed. "You've been working hard all day, and you're hungry."

Our apartment was on the second floor of a four-story apartment building at 159 South Eleventh Avenue, on the corner of Third Street, in Mount Vernon. It was a railroad flat—four square rooms lined up like the cars of a train. The kitchen had three doors: one to the main hallway and the other apartments, one to the back fire escape and the garbage shed below, and one to a tiny bathroom. A fourth doorway with no door led to my room, which opened through another empty doorway into my parents' bedroom and then to the living room beyond.

My brother Bill, thirteen years older than I, and my sister, Carol, almost seven years older, were both married and no longer lived at home.

My mother squeezed my father's forearm lightly, again urging, "Come on, honey." When he turned and stepped back into the doorway to the kitchen, my mother quickly glanced toward me and shook her head, signaling me to be quiet. The storm had passed.

I quietly slipped back under the covers and lay motionless on my back, every sense alert, my breathing shallow.

I heard their voices on the other side of the wall, but the words didn't register until I heard my mother say, "You're tired, honey. Let's go to sleep."

My father mumbled something as she helped him through my room and into theirs. I remained still as if paralyzed. I heard my father's body fall onto their bed, then silence. A few minutes later, my mother threaded through the darkness to my bed, sat at my side and placed her palm lightly on my forehead.

"I was really scared, Mom," I whispered.

"It's all right now," she whispered back. I couldn't see her tears in the darkness, but I knew they were there.

"How do you feel?" she asked.

"I'm OK, Mom," I answered.

"I love you," she said as she kissed me on the forehead.

She left my side and padded quietly to her own bedroom. Again, silence. I stared dry-eyed up and into the night. I rubbed my chest, which had begun to throb. My neck ached.

When my father rose a few hours later, he remembered nothing.

"What are you doing today?" he asked at the kitchen table.

I watched him pour a shot glass of Four Roses whiskey into black coffee.

"School, Daddy," I said.

"Yeah, school," he said. "Well, you'd better hurry up."

⤚

MUCH OF MY CHILDHOOD was like a dull rain punctured by noisy and unforgettable explosions of lightning. My most vivid memories are of brief and searing episodes. I lived in fear in an angry home.

I was no older than six or seven when I began to realize that I saw the world differently from nearly everyone around me. I kept my feelings to myself, but I made my choices in my own way. And I became defiant.

I remember one incident in particular, when I was nine years old. My mother was still at work, and Carol, who was still living with us at the time, was out buying groceries when my father surprised me. The kitchen door opened, and I was caught cold. It was too late to hide the evidence, which was right there in my lap, plain as could be. My father—drunk, his face flushed—reeled before me, glowering, menacing. My legs started to tremble. I knew I would be beaten. There could be no escape. My father had found me reading.

"Doin' that crap again!" he shouted.

"I'm sorry . . ." I tried to apologize, but the book, *Gulliver's Travels*, was slapped from my hands before I could finish my plea.

Then, terrified, I made a second mistake: I tried to stop the book from falling. When I reached for it, a hard, stinging punch to my shoulder knocked me from the chair.

My father could barely read—probably not as well as an average third-grader. His persistent rage about *my* reading frustrated me more than his other abuse, because I was drawn to books by curiosity and driven by need—an irresistible need to pretend that I was elsewhere. My mother, who wrote notes and reports for my father and did much of his reading for him, was acutely aware of the danger. Nevertheless, she encouraged me to read—as did another woman who lived nearby and who was becoming an increasingly important influence in my life.

As I raised myself from the floor, my father still standing over me, I said, "I'm sorry, Daddy. I won't do it again." But silently, secretly, I vowed that I would *never* stop reading.

CHAPTER 3

MOUNT VERNON lies just beyond the Bronx, the northern-most borough of New York City. It is a city of four square miles and seventy-five thousand people—and it is a city divided by a railroad cut.

We lived on the south side of the tracks—the "wrong side." The few short blocks of our neighborhood beat with the clank of metal parts, the din of human voices, the squealing of tires and the sounds of breaking glass. Eleventh Avenue was alive with smells, fresh and stale, and colors, from dull rust to fluorescent violet. It had several bars, two poolrooms, some gas stations, a fish market, dry cleaners, grocery and liquor stores, storefront churches and barbershops. There also were walk-up apartments and public housing projects. Good people lived there, sometimes only a thin plaster wall away from those who were not so good. Teenagers sang *a cappella* on the corners—songs made famous by such groups as the Platters, the Dimensions, the Shirelles and Mount Vernon's own Mello Kings. Basketball was played seriously on nearby playgrounds and sometimes raised to high art in bruising, brilliant games. One candy store was also a bookie joint where many, like my father, bet the daily numbers. Drunks, usually harmless, bobbed along late at night. A siren could signal a robbery, a rape, a birth, a death. Our neighborhood, with all its extremes, was a patchwork, a community unto itself.

Across the street, a few doors down from Cheatham Brothers Moving and Storage Company, was a two-story clapboard home with a large backyard. In this house lived Barry Williams, my best friend, with his older brothers, Otis and Keith, and their mother. Mrs. Williams was an educated person, a teacher in the New York City school system.

Barry and I loved to play basketball in his backyard. While I may have been more outwardly aggressive, Barry was a much better player. He was at least as competitive as I was, but his passion was concealed in the grace of a true athlete. In fact, he was more even-tempered than I in just about everything.

We had met in the neighborhood when we were four years old. Barry was by far the tallest child his age; I had to stretch to reach average. He was slender; I was heavier. Barry was black; I was white. He lived in a house; I lived in a tenement. His home was quiet; mine was not. What we shared, though, was so much larger: Both of us liked to read, to talk, to question. And, most important, we shared the unyielding encouragement of Barry's mother.

Mrs. Williams would begin a tale: "A long time ago, in the marsh country of England, there lived an orphan boy named Pip. One bleak evening he was visiting the graves of his parents. The sky darkened, and the wind blew, and the boy, afraid, started crying. Suddenly a deep voice roared, 'Keep still or I'll cut your throat!' and a terrible figure rose from among the tombstones."

"Then what happened?" one of us would ask.

"If you'd like to know," she'd tell us, smiling, "then read the book *Great Expectations,* by Charles Dickens." Of course, we couldn't wait to get to the library.

Sometimes she would call us into the house and ask us to help one of the students she tutored: "Boys, could you come and give me a hand?"

I was proud to be asked. So was Barry.

No neighborhood child could get within sight of Mrs. Williams without explaining his or her homework. If I happened to be over on a school night, Barry and I studied at the kitchen table.

When I'd become frustrated at some assignment, angry and ready to quit, she would reassure me, "You can do this, Walter." I believed Mrs. Williams, and I would persevere.

Barry had been identified early as a gifted student and now attended a private school. I went to a public school. I had failed the first grade before anyone recognized that I could not see the blackboard. An eye test confirmed that I needed glasses. My vision corrected, I led my classes academically in the second, third and fourth grades. Schoolwork seemed to come easier to me than it did to the other kids.

It was as if I could speak two languages, both English: I could street-talk on the corner about sports, fights, local gangs, music and movies. When I was in Barry's house, however, I spoke differently.

Sometime during those early years—despite the fact that I had been left back in first grade—Mrs. Williams concluded that I, like Barry, would be better off in a different school. One afternoon, she told my mother and father that she thought I had abilities that were not being recognized. She recommended that I leave Grimes Public School, which was only a block from our apartment, to enroll as a fifth-grade student in Immanuel Lutheran, a parochial school on the other side of town. She had examined the school's curriculum herself, found it healthy and liked the small class size.

Mrs. Williams had a way of making other people, child and adult alike, feel important. Invariably, she got her way. Even my father walked softly around Mrs. Williams. Maybe that's why he said OK.

Thus, I was enrolled as an Immanuel student, and my mother told me I'd be attending Immanuel Evangelical Lutheran Church.

I did as well academically in the fifth and sixth grades as I'd done in public school, and I became a starting player on the school basketball team. But I was not comfortable in the school or the church. By the seventh grade, I found myself stubbornly resisting and challenging the religious training: *Why did God make Jesus a Jew? Should we be Jewish too? Why does Jesus let people hurt each other? Why is God the Father so angry?* Answers only led me to ask more questions. I was unrelenting, and I flustered my teachers. I also felt like an outsider among my classmates.

I remember one Sunday morning in 1957 when I was seated, reluctantly, in a rear pew of Immanuel Evangelical Lutheran Church. The sermon seemed to lie like the early morning mist over a lake, the pastor's voice a gentle hum over the heavy silence in the room. As the service continued, the mist ever thickening, heads nodded, and my own eyes started to droop.

Involuntarily I chuckled, then snapped awake. The father of a schoolmate, sitting two rows ahead, turned at the sound and gave me a stern look. I averted my eyes.

I could feel the warmth of the heavyset woman who sat next to me, her bulk squeezing me tightly into the corner of the pew. I smiled uncomfortably at her.

She frowned.

I stopped smiling.

I sat quietly for what seemed an eternity—a peace that in truth probably lasted no more than twenty seconds. *Is my leg falling asleep?* I moved my toes. No. No pain there. My mind wandered again, and I found myself studying some of the parishioners and wondering silently, *Why do you come here?* I saw more heads nod.

Why am I here?

To be a Lutheran, I reminded myself—like most of the other boys and girls in my class. I knew I would be confirmed in two Sundays, after I had passed an oral exam scheduled to be given in a few days. My classmates and I had dutifully, if not enthusiastically, studied our catechisms and memorized endless questions and answers.

I worried, though, that the questions were not *my* questions, and I had no answers. After all the instruction both in school and in church—all the hours of listening, reading and listening again—I was profoundly troubled. Worse, at thirteen years old, I was unable to articulate to my teachers and the minister how deeply troubled I was.

My neighborhood was a tossed salad of colors and languages, but all of the children played together. Some of my friends were Catholic, others Jewish. Many were black Baptists. *Why*, I wanted to know, *don't Catholics go to heaven? Or Jews? Or Baptists?* When I raised these questions with my teacher, he assured me that I had been shown the one true and sure path to redemption, and I was even encouraged to spread the word. That wasn't the answer I had hoped for. What's more, my mother, older brother and sister had been raised Protestant, though not Lutheran—and the closest my father ever came to any church was at weddings and funerals. *What about them?*

This was unsettling. *Are my family and many of my friends damned? Why? Is God unfair?* I didn't understand.

Like apples slowly bobbing in a pail of water, more heads nodded among the congregation. *Why am I here?* I asked myself again. *Do I believe?*

The question startled me: *Do I believe?* I was sure I was crossing a line, a very dangerous line. We had been warned about just such a moment—how terribly tempting Satan could be, how he could raise doubts. I understood I was risking my very soul. Like a moth, I circled the flame. I tried thinking about something else. The harder I tried, the harder it became. The moth drew closer to the light.

Sitting in the church, the minister's voice a soft hiss in the still air, I silently asked myself, "Is there a God?"

The question frightened me.

I waited.

Nothing.

Again I asked, "Is there a God?"

No response.

I could stand it no longer. "If there's a God," I prayed, "strike me dead!" I shuddered. The moth dove into the flame.

Squeezing my eyes tightly shut, I awaited the worst.

Seconds passed.

I raised my right eyelid slightly, then opened both eyes wide.

I was safe! The moth had escaped the flame.

When I prayed again, it was with more, not less, confidence: "I don't know whether you're there, God, but I do know what I'm going to do. No matter how I'm punished, I'm not going through with this."

The next hour stands out as one of the most anxious of my childhood. The walk home was painful. I couldn't seem to get my thoughts together. I knew I had to tell my parents I was not going to be a Lutheran—this after they had spent money, money they didn't have, to send me to a parochial school affiliated with the Lutheran Church. What would I say? What would they say? Or do? I was sure my mother would listen, but my father . . . well, I didn't know. Would I be beaten? Would I be told I *had* to go through with the confirmation? I feared that most of all, because I realized I would disobey if they insisted, no matter the consequence.

For several seconds, I stood outside the door to our apartment. *What am I going to do?*

When I finally walked in, my mother was setting the table for dinner.

"Hi, honey," she said.

"Hi, Mom. Where's Daddy?"

"Sleeping."

"I've got something I want to say," I began, "and it's this: I don't want to be confirmed in that church. I don't believe any of it, Mom."

I continued at length, honestly answering the questions she raised, leaving out only the part about asking God to strike me dead. I told her I did not belong in that congregation. She wanted to know if I'd like to join a different church. I assured her I would not.

My mother was quiet for a few minutes. "Are you sure?" she finally asked.

"I really am."

"Let me talk to your father first," she told me, her decision made.

"What do you think he'll say?"

"He'll support you."

"How can you be so sure?"

"I'm sure."

She was right. To my relief, my father—who had read no Scripture, who had sought no preacher's advice and who had attended no church—was matter-of-fact, neither angry nor pleased. When I told him I was sure I didn't want to be confirmed, he simply said, "Then that's your decision."

The next morning, I nervously asked to speak with the minister. "Reverend," I stammered, "I don't want to be confirmed."

"Why?" he asked, his eyebrows raised as if he had heard a strange sound from another room.

I hesitated.

"I don't believe . . ." I began.

"In *God?*" he interrupted, his eyes widening.

"In what I've been taught," I said.

He was a kind, sympathetic man, and he talked for a solid ten minutes, repeatedly assuring me that doubt was not unusual.

I listened respectfully.

Finally, he asked, "Are you sure?"

"Yes, sir," I said.

"Maybe next year," the minister told me.

I never returned to that church, and I don't think I ever saw him again.

LIFE BECAME MORE complicated for me back at Immanuel. A new teacher had taken over my class at the beginning of seventh grade, and he and I waged a quiet war. He was determined to change my attitude, which he found rebellious, and my appearance, which he found objectionable. Our struggle came to a head early one morning in the middle of the school year.

I believed all eyes were on me, burning right through the back of my neck as surely as if they were spotlights. I wanted to scream or cry or die. My heart beat so loudly in my ears that I was sure others could hear it too.

The teacher had ordered me to remove my shirt and stand at my desk. What bothered him was that I had my shirt collar up, an adolescent style in the Fifties. He was going to make an example of me before my classmates.

"Take off your shirt!" he ordered.

I promised not to turn my collar up again.

"I've caught you twice," he said, striding to my desk.

In my neighborhood, teenagers wore motorcycle jackets, greased their hair, talked tough. Immanuel was on the north side of town—the "right side" of the tracks—in a section called Fleetwood. I crossed the tracks to go home every night, home to a block where all the kids wore their collars up.

"Take it off!" the teacher ordered, hovering over me.

He was a tall man, and his body blocked any chance that I might have had to run. Somebody giggled.

"Please," I pleaded.

"Now!"

I unbuttoned the front of my shirt.

"Hurry up!"

I opened my cuffs and slipped the shirt off, draping it behind me on my chair. Several students giggled.

"Stand up!"

I stood up.

The teacher, who had been standing beside my desk, marched back to the front of the classroom. He had been bullying me all year because I was different—or at least seemed different because of my clothes. Having forgotten to turn my collar down, I had given him the opening he'd been looking for.

I stood alone.

"Turn to page . . . ," he began, ignoring me.

I heard my heart beating even louder in my ears, and the heat at the base of my neck was becoming unbearable because my worst secret had been revealed for all to see: My undershirt had holes—holes that proved I was poor, proved I was a south-sider unworthy of the north-siders in the room.

Maybe it was seconds, maybe it was minutes, before I reached for my shirt and began to put it back on.

"I didn't tell you to move," the teacher said from the front of the class. I ignored him, continued to button my shirt and sat down. The bell rang for recess before he could get to me.

"Wait!" he ordered. Everyone stopped.

"Just Walter," he amended.

One or two students hesitated by the door, hoping to hear what he was going to say. "Move," he told them.

"You are going to learn to listen to me," he said.

I was silent.

"Now go to recess."

I walked to the door, turned back to the teacher and called out his name.

"Yes?" he replied.

"Go to hell!" I said, my eyes filling with tears.

CHAPTER 4

MY MOTHER WAS SUMMONED to appear before Immanuel's school board, which wanted to expel me immediately. She pleaded with the board members to allow me to remain as a student until June, when, she assured them, she would transfer me elsewhere.

Finally, they agreed to her plea, but they also made it clear that my expulsion was merely suspended, not lifted. The smallest infraction on my part, she was warned firmly, would trigger the punishment.

"I want you to give me your word," she said to me after the meeting, "that, *no matter what*, you'll obey the teacher."

"I promise," I told her, and I meant it: My mother had been humiliated by some of the board members' questions about my attitude, and the guilt I felt was excruciating. I made no attempt to defend myself, although I was enraged by the unfairness and cruelty of the incident.

For my mother's sake, I swallowed my fury. I was calm—even when my father started up.

I remember how the taste of metal appeared in my mouth when he began to beat me, and I also remember that, for the first time, I did not feel the pain. I knew not to cry: Tears would only provoke more punishment. But that wasn't it. I did not seem to hurt. Nor was there a need for me to cry. It was as if I were an observer, disembodied, watching as my father punched and shouted.

I dreaded returning to Immanuel the next day. It was a very long bicycle ride across the city that morning. I was determined to keep my word, as I had promised my mother, *no matter what*.

Minutes after I had taken my seat, I sensed something new. I noticed that the teacher made no attempt to provoke me with a remark about my appearance or demeanor. To the contrary, when he called on me later in the hour, his tone was even and polite. During recess, a classmate asked, "What did you do to the teacher?"

"Nothing," I said, and the discussion ended. The rest of the day, to my extreme relief, passed easily.

Mrs. Williams, of course, wanted to know what had happened in school. She listened carefully as I described the shirt-collar incident. Although I was embarrassed, it was easy to speak with her.

"Where will you be going to school in September?" she asked.

"I'll be starting eighth grade at Washington Junior High School," I told her, "with my friends from the neighborhood."

"Well, we'll see," she said.

A few days later, with my mother's permission, Mrs. Williams arranged for me to take a series of tests over several hours at Windward, a private school in White Plains, New York. I was then interviewed by a teacher, Terry Cade, and by the principal, Dr. Meyer Rabban, who also was a psychologist.

During the tests, I acted as if I didn't care one way or the other about going to Windward. After Miss Cade described for me how students studied there in open classrooms and at their own speed, however, I secretly wanted to attend. I pretended otherwise, because I didn't think I had a chance. I was sure I would be rejected because I was being expelled from another school. Dr. Rabban had asked me to explain what had happened at Immanuel, and I had, in detail.

Thus, I was surprised when the principal called my mother the following week at Gimbel's Department Store, where she worked as a switchboard supervisor, to tell her that I had been accepted at Windward. What's more, I had qualified for a scholarship, and Dr. Rabban offered to help find someone to drive me to and from school starting in September.

With this promise of change, I finished the school year at Immanuel without further incident, although inside I was in turmoil.

I found myself becoming increasingly angry. Undoubtedly, much of my rage grew out of the abuse and fear I lived with every day at home. But I had a deeper frustration: I didn't seem to belong anywhere. I was not *normal*. It wasn't so much that I looked different from other members of my family or dressed differently from my classmates; I *was* different. And the aching feelings of loneliness and doubt, which I kept to myself, hurt more than my father's frequent beatings.

I had struggled since I was six or seven years old to figure out whom I could depend on, whom I could trust. By fourteen, I began to ask myself another question in earnest: *Who am I?* I was Walter to my friends on Third Street, to my teachers at school and to my parents at home. I knew, though, that this boy called Walter spoke and acted very differently in all three places—and felt complete in none.

One night, just after I turned fourteen, still stands out in my mind. My mother asked me to walk to the telephone booth across the street from our tenement to make a call to my brother. We had no telephone at the time. I can't remember the message or our discussion, but I clearly recall the incident because, when I replaced the receiver, I noticed blood on my hand. I touched my face with the other hand and found more blood. I wasn't bleeding, but whoever had used the phone before me had been hurt or wounded.

I ran across the street, bounded up the stairs to our apartment and hurried to the kitchen sink to wash the blood from my face before my mother could see it. About an hour later, I sat alone on the front stoop and wondered about the mysterious person whose blood had covered my face.

Then I became incensed.

I'm getting out of here, I promised myself. And, for the first time, I meant it.

ON THE STREET, I fought frequently. Sometimes I fought to protect myself or to help a friend. Mainly, though, I fought because I was afraid, and I won most encounters. But unlike my brother Bill, who was a talented boxer, I didn't win because of superior athletic skill. I won because I had learned at a very young age to land the first punch in a fight, and—because of my father's violence—I could absorb considerable punishment and still prevail.

I also cursed loudly on the street, broke rules and made minor trouble with some of my neighborhood friends. Many had family situations not much different from my own, some worse. More important, though, I could depend on my friends. I could trust them.

One night I was playing pool at Teen Town, a youth center located near the edge of the railroad cut that split Mount Vernon. Another teenager, named George, insisted that it was his turn to play.

"No, it's mine," I said.

Seven or eight other teenagers were drawn to the noise and started to form a circle, which grew steadily. They coaxed George, egging him on and leaving him no choice but to assert himself or be humiliated. No sooner would he respond than the catcalls and the prodding would turn on me: "You gonna take *that*, Anderson? I wouldn't take *that*!" I'm sure that neither George nor I wanted the inevitable fight, but we were too scared to admit we were scared.

"Give me the stick!" George ordered, reaching for the pool cue I held in my hand.

"You want this?" I said, glancing toward the pool cue. "I'll give it to you . . . ," and I brought it up as you would a baseball bat. "Still want it, George?"

Before he could answer, the cue was snatched from my hands by a counselor, an older teenager, who barked at us, "Cool off! Now neither one of you can play." Then he ordered George and me to walk in opposite directions.

The circle of onlookers broke up and disappeared, disappointed. Relieved, though I tried not to let it show, I headed to another room to get a soda. There, I got into a game of gin rummy with a tall boy named Donald and his friend Roy. We played for about a half hour, then decided to leave. As we rounded the corner at Second Avenue, heading for Third Street, we heard a shout, "Hey, Anderson!"

It was George and four friends, each a couple of years older than us. They laughed and seemed to be whispering instructions to him.

"Hey, punk, wait up!" George shouted as he and his friends drew closer. With each of their steps, my heart pounded harder, my throat dried, my stomach tightened.

"You staying?" I asked Donald and Roy.

"Yeah."

"Thanks," I said, and meant it, respecting their courage in backing up someone they hardly knew.

"You with him?" one of George's friends asked.

"That's right," Donald replied, his voice even. Roy nodded and then said, "Why are you askin'?"

The teenager looked hard into Roy's eyes, which stared back, unblinking. George's friend hesitated, looked toward one of his companions, then suggested, "Let them have it out."

Everyone else took a couple of steps back, leaving George and me a few feet apart and facing each other. One of his friends stepped forward and whispered in George's ear. It was a dark, cool November evening, the streetlights yellow on the pavement. George and I were about the same size. If he wasn't "carrying"—no knives or belts or other weapons—it would be a fair fight, I thought.

"You better take off your glasses, *four-eyes*," George said.

"It don't matter," I replied. "You won't touch 'em."

"Take 'em off!" George ordered.

George clearly wanted to talk, not fight, but his friends were going to have none of it. They came to see blood.

"Nail him, George!" someone shouted.

"Cut 'im up, cut 'im up!"

"Break his glasses," said the teenager who had whispered to George. Donald and Roy watched like silent sentries. George stepped toward me.

"That's it! Go get 'im, George!"

He came at me, both arms wide and flailing. But rather than step back, as George probably expected I would, I stepped forward and threw a straight right hand—a move my brother had taught me. It caught George in the neck. He was off balance, and we came together so suddenly that the force flipped him backward. His head sounded like a sack of flour dropped on a linoleum floor when it slapped the pavement. He didn't stir. His eyes were glazed and only half open.

"George, you all right?" I asked nervously, leaning down. He made no sound. "You all right?" I asked again.

"Is he breathin'?" Donald asked.

I looked up. George's "friends," sensing real trouble, already had begun to walk away.

George finally stirred, mumbling, "My head hurts . . . my head really hurts."

The three of us helped him up. After a few steps, George was able to walk unaided, though a large knot had swelled at the base of his skull.

"Thanks," George said.

"Hey, I'm sorry," I said, my relief genuine.

"Me too," he replied.

"We knew *you* were sorry," Roy said, prompting all of us, even George, to laugh.

AT WINDWARD, Terry Cade was better than her word. Like Mrs. Williams, she was patient with me when I became frustrated—a feeling I experienced less and less as the year went on. She was a *guide* to knowledge, someone who suggested ideas to consider, books to read, life to experience.

While some of our course material was discussed in class, we studied as individuals and helped to design our own homework assignments. This meant that we did not compete academically. The scores I had received in public and parochial schools always seemed to be taken from a pool of grades: a few high, most average, and a few low. At Windward, I actually was measured by my progress against myself, which caused me to work harder.

Many of my fellow students were from prosperous families in Westchester County, far wealthier than anyone I had known before. I was insecure around them, and I was jealous of where they were able to live, how they were able to dress, what they were able to buy.

As students, few at Windward would have been called "average." Most were either fast- or slow-learners. With Immanuel fresh in my mind, I was very careful: I did not want my classmates to get to know me. I kept to myself, and I studied. Occasionally, I would be challenged at recess with a cutting comment from another male student, but I would not respond. Of course, I'd fantasize about the boy making the same remark to me on Third Street. Usually, in the fantasy, I could see myself punching him out. More than the insult, I wanted to punish my tormentor just for being rich.

One afternoon I arrived home, looked in the mirror and discovered that my collar was up. It must have been up throughout the school day—but nothing had happened. I decided to talk with Miss Cade about collars.

She asked why my collar, up or down, was important to me. I told her about my experience at Immanuel. That led to a longer discussion, followed by many more talks. I trusted Miss Cade and increasingly looked forward to speaking with her.

One day Miss Cade told me she thought I would become a writer.

"Why?" I asked.

She explained that the essays I had written at Windward demonstrated both a talent for expression and a deep desire to communicate. She said it was obvious that books excited me, and she reminded me how passionately I talked about authors.

I confided for the first time that I was secretly writing a novel at home called *Hanover Hill*, a love story about a black man and a white woman. I said I was inspired by the people I saw around me, as a white kid in a mostly black neighborhood, and I told her that writing was very difficult for me.

"Why do you write if it's difficult for you?" she asked.

"Because I feel free when I write," I replied. "And the people I write about are as real to me as almost anyone I know—I can hear them talk. Besides, it's the only way I can find out what happens next."

CHAPTER 5

WHEN I WAS a little boy and my sister was a teenager, she would be assigned to watch over me on Friday nights. That's when my mother would play bingo at Mount St. Michael's in the Bronx. My father would either be drinking somewhere or working the night shift as an emergency lineman. On the nights he was working, Carol would supply me with soda and potato chips, then slip out to meet a boy my father had ordered her not to see because, like all boys, he was not "good enough" for *his* daughter. If my father drove by in his Con Edison truck to check on her, I was coached by Carol to say that she was at the grocery store buying milk and had *just* left.

It worked for a while.

One night, though, my father caught Carol walking by Teen Town, which was several blocks away. He tossed her in his truck, then ordered her to stay inside when he parked in front of our tenement.

Invariably, when my father drove by our building, he would shine the spotlight from his truck directly at our front windows—and we were required to raise the shades and wave to him. When my mother was home, she did the waving. So I was surprised to see my father suddenly materialize in our apartment that Friday evening. He had come in quietly—and he was smiling.

"Where's your sister?" he asked me, setting his trap.

"Oh," I replied cheerfully, "Carol *just* went to the store to get milk, Daddy. She'll be right back."

"Look out the front window," he said.

I opened the shades and looked down. Carol stared back at me from the cab of the truck. She raised her hands and shrugged.

That night he beat both of us—but, to our astonishment, the beatings were mild.

"I thought it would be a lot worse," I later confided to Carol.

"Me too," she agreed.

"What do you think happened?"

"I don't know," she said. "He seemed *pleased*."

"No," I said, "he was *happy*."

"It was like he was glad he was right."

"Yeah," I said. "He was very glad."

MY SISTER AND I shared secrets for as long as I can remember. Thus, in the spring of 1959, I confided to Carol that I didn't think I would be returning to Windward in the fall.

"What did you do this time?" she asked, worried. "I thought you liked Windward."

"I like Windward OK," I said. "But I finished the eighth-grade assignments before Christmas, and now I'll finish the rest of the ninth grade in a couple of weeks. Windward doesn't have a tenth grade."

Carol shook her head.

"I don't know how you do it," she said. "No one in the family can learn things like you do. Hell, even when you get in trouble, you're smart in school. You had good grades when they expelled you from Immanuel . . ."

"I'm *not* getting thrown out," I interrupted.

"And I bet you go to Davis," she finished.

Mount Vernon had two public high schools: Thomas Edison, which was mainly vocational; and A. B. Davis, which was more academic. Carol had attended Edison before she got married, and Bill had graduated from Davis before enlisting in the Navy.

"I'll probably go to Davis," I said.

"Maybe you should ask Mrs. Williams what she thinks."

"I will," I promised.

MRS. WILLIAMS immediately began making other plans. After speaking with my mother, she lobbied two elite private high schools, Westminster and Cherry Lawn, both in Connecticut.

"Walter," she told me one afternoon, "I have wonderful news. Westminster *and* Cherry Lawn have encouraged you to apply for admission."

"What does that mean?"

"That means they *want* you to apply," she said, "and if all goes as I hope it will, you'll get a scholarship and live on campus."

A few hours earlier, I had been sitting alone in our apartment, with the smell of garbage wafting through the kitchen window and cockroaches scurrying across the cracked linoleum floor. *How many times*, I wondered, *have I been beaten in my room?* I knew I didn't want to belong to this place—but, I asked myself, do I belong at Westminster or Cherry Lawn? Do I belong with the neatly dressed, smiling students I saw in the school pictures? I stood up and examined myself in the mirror. My hair was long; my shoes were engineer boots; my topcoat was a motorcycle jacket; my pants were jeans held up by a black garrison belt. Outside, on the corner, the other kids looked like me.

So, when we spoke later, I didn't give Mrs. Williams the reply I'm sure she expected. Instead, I thanked her and asked, "Can I think about this for a couple of days?"

It took me that long to screw up the courage—and marshal the will—to tell Mrs. Williams candidly what I felt. I told her that I wasn't going to complete the application process for either Westminster or Cherry Lawn. I told her I wanted to go back to school with my friends, and I assured her that she could trust me to do well.

"Walter," she said, "if you're worried about being turned down . . ."

"No," I stopped her, "I'm worried about being *accepted*."

I was near tears when Mrs. Williams finally conceded. No beating ever hurt me as much as disappointing this woman who so believed in me.

IN MY SECOND WEEK at A. B. Davis High School, I cut my first class.

My brother and my father had gotten into an argument the night before. After my brother left in a huff to return to his own apartment across town, my father, still annoyed at Bill, began to beat *me*. This time, though, I hit back—once. Then my father punched me so hard that I actually saw flashes of light. He beat me severely.

The next day, I ached all over. *To hell with school*, I thought. I decided to hang out with my friends. By the following May, I had cut classes scores of times, and I rarely was caught.

≈

ONE SUNDAY NIGHT, shortly before ten o'clock, I typed the last sentence of *Hanover Hill* on an old Remington portable typewriter and felt triumphant. The last chapter had been especially difficult to write because, when I started the book, I thought it would have a happy ending. As I secretly labored night after night, though, I discovered that this particular story, to be true, had to be a tragedy: It was about an interracial romance that ended in separation.

I gave the manuscript, about 150 pages, to my mother. It took her three days to finish reading. We were in the living room together when she turned the last page. She was crying.

"Is it that bad?" I asked, smiling nervously.

"No," she said, "it's beautiful. It's a wonderful story. This man and woman don't exist, but they seem so real. What are you going to do with this?"

"I'm going to send it to a publisher."

"Do you think they'll publish it?" she asked.

"Why not? It made *you* cry."

THE FOLLOWING WEEK, I packaged *Hanover Hill*, walked to the post office a few blocks away and mailed my manuscript to a publishing house.

Then I waited. And waited.

Finally, after about two months, I received a package from the publisher. I trembled as I held it. *This is it*, I thought. *They're going to publish my novel.*

I tore the wrapping. It was my manuscript, and enclosed with it was a form letter advising me that *Hanover Hill* had been rejected.

My eyes filled as I placed the manuscript back in its wrapper. I carried the package through the back door, down the fire escape and to the enclosed garbage shed behind our tenement. I found a can that was only half filled and tossed my novel onto a filthy brown paper bag, along with any dreams of writing my way out of this neighborhood. Fortunately, another ticket out of Mount Vernon would soon arrive.

MISS LORRAINE ROUGET, my homeroom teacher, made an announcement to the class one morning. "The Vermont Farm Volunteer Program," she said, "is looking for students to work on farms during the summer. You have to be at least fifteen. If anybody is interested, you'll get room and board and earn fifty-five dollars a month." When class was dismissed, I picked up an application from the principal's office.

Every May or June, from the time I was five years old until I was fourteen, I had been driven upstate to Malta, New York, to stay with my Aunt Phil and Uncle George to help during the summer haying season. Their farm was a little larger than a hundred acres. I may have been the only kid on Third Street who could drive a tractor, plow a field, strip a cow's milk, build a fence and find my way through woods. I'm certain I was the only teenager on my block who had shoveled tons of manure into a spreader over ten summers. And, with patient instruction and encouragement from my older cousins, George and Philip, I had learned how to fish competently before I was ten and how to safely care for, store and fire a rifle.

.However hard the work, I cherished the farm. For three months every year, I was 160 miles out of range of my father's punches. That would have been enough incentive to get away for the summer, but there was so much more. I loved seeing my aunt, my uncle, my cousins and my grandmother, Lillian Crolly, a gifted storyteller who lived with them on the farm.

Now, though, I wouldn't be going there to help out anymore. My uncle had been forced to sell off his small herd of dairy cows. "The middlemen made all the money to begin with," he complained, "and big business killed the little farmer by dropping milk prices."

I knew I would miss my relatives and the farm. What made matters worse, the tension between me and my father was escalating. I was determined not to spend the summer of 1960 at home. Fortunately, the Whitcomb family of Essex Junction, Vermont, outside Burlington, selected me for the farm volunteer program soon after reading my application.

On the night I was to catch a Greyhound to Burlington, my Uncle Bill Thiele drove me to the Port Authority Bus Terminal in Manhattan with my Aunt Florence and my mother. The Thieles also lived in our tenement with their son and daughter. They left to return home about fifteen minutes before I was to board, and I found myself a seat in the waiting room. Seconds later, a pudgy, gray-haired man about my height plopped down next to me.

He asked where I was heading.

"Burlington, Vermont," I told him.

"How much money do you have on you?" he asked.

"Why?" I replied gruffly.

"No, no," he said coolly, responding to my hostile tone, "I'm only asking because I thought you might want this jewelry." He pointed to a gold ring on his pinkie. It had a shiny black stone in its center.

"I'd let you have it for fifty dollars," he said.

"I don't have fifty dollars."

"Do you have *fifteen* dollars?" he asked.

I had ten dollars and a one-way bus ticket. I did not want to surrender either. "Look," I said, "I don't want your ring."

"I think you do," he said, his voice hard now, threatening: "Buy the ring, boy."

My stomach constricted. A memory flashed.

FOUR YEARS EARLIER, I had been threatened by another man. I was eleven at the time and had skipped school to go to Manhattan to buy an

identification bracelet at a novelty store. After the purchase, I walked to
the subway in Times Square to make the trip home and suddenly found
myself confused amid a crush of people: Which train? Which track?

"Mister," I asked the man in the token booth, "which train do I take
to get to 241st Street and White Plains Road in the Bronx?"

He pointed to a stairwell, then shouted, "Remember to change trains
at 180th Street!"

Almost as he spoke, a construction worker wearing heavy tan work
boots, a faded denim shirt and jeans tapped my elbow, surprising me.
"Here," he said. "I'll show you. I'm going the same way."

I was uneasy. His cheeks were crisscrossed with tiny jagged scars, his
eyebrows were scarred in ragged sections, his ears were cauliflowered,
and he had a large scar across the bridge of his flattened nose and
another slicing both his upper and lower lips.

"I'm a fighter," he said as he followed me into a crowded subway car.
I nodded.

He was sandy-haired, probably in his mid-thirties, and I could see
the muscles of his arms flexing through his shirt.

"You like fighting?" he asked.

I nodded again.

"Like me to teach you?"

"No," I said. "I just like to watch boxing and wrestling sometimes."

I could sense something, feel it, smell it. This was a dangerous man,
a man I had to get away from.

"Thanks for helping me," I said, "but I'm all right now. You can get
off at your station if you want to."

"Why don't you get off with me?" he asked.

"What?"

"Yeah," he said, "you can come to my apartment and watch television with me."

I knew not to panic, though panic is what I felt. I looked down the
car, still crowded as we approached the 180th Street station. *Good*, I

thought, *I can make a scene if I have to.* My stomach ached. *Just don't panic.* I remembered that my parents thought I was in school, and the school principal thought I was home. No one knew where I was. *Don't think about it*, I told myself. *Just don't panic.*

"No," I said, "I've got to get home—but thanks again for getting me on the right train."

The doors opened at 180th Street. I stepped out onto the platform, the only child in a crowd of several dozen adults; the man stepped off with me.

"Do you know," he asked, "what train to catch from here?"

"Yeah," I said, "thanks."

He started talking about his boxing career, whom he had fought, how he had gotten cheated, how he couldn't get good fights anymore, how he had become a sparring partner and how, to earn "regular money," he worked as a construction laborer.

I saw my train approaching the station. Again he asked, "Sure you don't want to come to my apartment?"

"I can't," I said, and stepped into the subway car. He followed me. *Just don't panic.*

As the train screeched along, station signs speeding by, his tone changed.

"Why won't you come with me?"

It didn't sound like a question.

I knew the 241st Street station was only a few minutes ahead, but I was trapped. The fighter stood between me and the door. Only a handful of other riders were in the car.

"C'mon," he argued, his tone harsh. "Let's go watch television in my apartment!"

Although he spoke loudly, angrily, the few people in the car seemed not to hear a word. An older man looked away when I glanced toward him. I was on my own, and I knew it. *Just don't panic.*

"I can't," I said.

"Don't you like me?"

"Sure."

"Then why not?"

I tried to be steady, but my voice trembled anyway: "I have . . . to go home."

He placed his hand on my shoulder and squeezed. I could feel my legs weaken. My stomach tensed. I wanted to cry, to scream. *Just don't panic.*

"I know about boys like you," he said. "What do you want?"

"Nothing," I told him.

"Then how come you went to Times Square?"

"Only to buy this," I said. As I lifted my left arm to show him the identification bracelet, I could see through the subway window that the train was pulling into the 241st Street station.

"Let me see that," he said, grabbing my wrist.

The doors opened. *Just don't panic.* My pulse was racing. *Think. Think.*

"Hey!" I yelled.

The unexpected scream startled him. Before he could react, I wrenched my wrist away, ducked under his arm and tried to leap through the doors behind him. Losing my balance as I jumped, I stumbled onto the subway platform on my hands and knees, my eyeglasses falling from my face.

Then I panicked.

My glasses had landed almost at the feet of a man who was sweeping litter with a broom and a long-handled dustpan. He was an older man with white hair, and he was black.

"Help me," I pleaded, sobbing and shouting. "Help me!" I threw my arms around his legs and tightly clutched my hands together.

The fighter, swearing, stepped off the train and reached for me.

"That's my little brother," he said.

"I'm not!" I screamed.

"Outta here, or I'll split your punk head wide open!" the old man threatened, raising his dustpan high. The fighter cursed.

"Call a cop!" the old man shouted toward the platform steps.

The fighter cursed again, then turned and stepped back onto the train.

"You OK, boy?" the old man asked.

I nodded.

"Did he hurt you?"

"No," I said, sniffling. "He didn't get a chance."

I picked up my glasses.

"Thank you," I said.

"You sure you're OK?"

"Yeah," I told the old man. "I just want to go home now."

He patted me on the shoulder. "Go on, boy," he said.

I FORCED MYSELF to take a closer look at the man who was now pressing me to buy his ring. The skin of his face was pasty, fleshy, and it sagged. His body was puffy and soft. He was about my height, only much heavier. *I'm not an eleven-year-old boy playing hooky,* I thought to myself, *and this guy's no fighter. If I have to, I can hurt him. Damn, we're sitting in the Port Authority Bus Terminal! Is he stupid enough to try something in this room? If he's that desperate, and I have to fight him, when the cops find out that I have a bus ticket—and he doesn't have one, I'll bet— they'll believe me!*

Now I was angry.

"Pretty soon," I said flatly, "they're going to announce my bus, and I'm going to board it. And I won't have your ring with me. Beat it."

He slouched as though he were a balloon that had deflated.

"How about five dollars?" he asked.

"Forget it," I told him.

A few minutes later, safely seated aboard the Greyhound bus rolling out of the city on its way to Vermont, I was pleased with myself. The trip was off to a good start. I had handled things.

Slowly, the lights of the highway passed in the long night, and I began to wonder what the summer would bring.

CHAPTER 6

THE WHITCOMBS' FARM covered more than five hundred acres in the lush rolling hills leading to Vermont's Green Mountains, and the family—with help from working hands like myself—milked four times as many cows as Uncle George had ever had on his farm.

Mr. Whitcomb was as solid a man as I've known, a man whose workday was never done: Oh, how he raged against the dying of the light! White-haired, aged and slowed by the unavoidable passing of the years, he nonetheless worked the long, hard hours of a farmer alongside his two adult sons and, in the summer of 1960, alongside me.

I wrote a letter to my mother once a week, often describing—boasting—how I'd rise in the dark before dawn, help with the first milking, go to the fields and load bales of hay all day onto tractor-drawn wagons in the sun, help again with the second milking, load more hay and go to bed about ten o'clock. I reported that everyone on the farm worked those long hours six days a week and even worked on Sundays, all of us stopping about eleven in the morning. Once every four weeks, I would slip forty of the fifty-five dollars I had earned into the letter. "Put it away for me," I'd write, "so that when I return to Mount Vernon at the end of August, I'll be able to buy clothes and have some money for school."

I UNDERSTOOD A DAIRY farm. It's raining: *Milk the cows*. It's hailing: *Milk the cows*. It's a hurricane: *Milk the cows*. I've got the flu: *Milk the cows*. My elbow got mangled in the machinery: *Milk the cows*. It's the Fourth of July: *Milk the cows*. It's Christmas: *Milk the cows*. The sun will rise and the sun will set—and dairy cows will be milked twice a day. *Every* day.

When Mr. Whitcomb saw that I kept pace with the older farmhands without complaint, he told his wife that I was a good lad. She confided his comment to me, knowing that her husband was not a fellow given easily to praise.

Mrs. Whitcomb herself was a generous and ebullient soul, cheery and light. She had met her husband, to whom she was totally devoted, when he served in the military in Europe during World War I, and she retained her Scottish lilt: "See you in the mornin' light, Walter."

Not long after I arrived at the farm, Mrs. Whitcomb asked if I'd like to go to church on Sunday.

"No," I said, "I don't want to go to church."

I think the finality of my reply surprised her; it certainly surprised me.

"I'm sorry," I added quickly. "Thank you for asking. It's just that I'm not all that comfortable in church."

She smiled but stayed silent. I could *feel* the question that she did not ask.

"Mrs. Whitcomb," I told her, "I think I believe in God—at least sometimes I think I do."

She told me I didn't have to explain myself.

"I wish I *could* explain myself," I confided, "but the truth is, I'm not sure of what I'm for. I'm only sure of what I'm *not* for."

"I don't understand," she said.

"Neither do I," I admitted.

AN OLDER FARMHAND, a grizzled and crotchety hermit of a man about the same age as Mr. Whitcomb, ignored me for several weeks but then slowly started to acknowledge my presence.

One morning he nodded in my direction, and I nodded back. A couple of days later, he spoke to me.

"Mornin'," he said.

"Good morning," I replied.

Thus, a dialogue gradually began. To my delight, I discovered he was a compelling storyteller, and I learned to listen quietly and patiently: Questions were to be asked *after* and not during a tale.

I remember one story in particular:

A hired hand—a family man with a young son—worked at a farm not far from us. He labored for a farmer who was a nasty piece of work, an alcoholic who bullied his one worker unmercifully and cheated the poor man whenever possible by docking his pay for mistakes.

There was little the hand could do about the situation. His nine-year-old son also did chores, as did his wife, but they were not paid. Working at a farm was all the man knew—so, with a family to support, he endured the abuse.

Worse, the farmer regularly complained to whomever would listen about the hand's imagined failures—the farmer's version of events, of course, always contrived to prove his own patience and generosity.

Neighbors were not fooled by the fabrications, but neither did they interfere.

Then, one afternoon, the farmer went too far.

The hand, while carrying two filled buckets to the milk shed—with the farmer drunk and loudly berating him at his side—spilled some milk. Enraged, the farmer grabbed an axe handle and severely beat him in front of the man's small son.

The hand could not work again. His spine had been shattered, and he was paralyzed from the waist down. Unfortunately, the child who witnessed the beating was too frightened and confused to testify. The farmer thus was able to successfully claim in court that he had only defended himself. The man's family, penniless, was left to struggle.

"A couple of weeks later," the old storyteller continued, "that farmer was found hanging from a tree near his barn, his body beaten black and blue."

"Who did it?" I asked.

"No one knows for sure, but they say vigilantes pulled him from his farm, whipped him good and hanged him."

"What happened to the farmhand and his family?"

"They were taken in by the community," he replied, "and I understand they're all right now."

"The farmer got what he deserved," I observed.

"Ever know anybody that mean?" he asked me.

"No," I replied coolly.

CHAPTER 7

ALMOST THE INSTANT I knocked on the door to the apartment, I could hear my mother shout, "Walter!" She quickly opened the door, stood on her toes, threw her arms around my neck, kissed my cheek and squeezed me. My father, seated at the kitchen table, smiled and asked, "How was the bus trip?"

"It was good," I said. "It's a long ride. I think I slept a couple of hours on the bus."

"Good," he said. "How did you like the summer?"

"I liked it a lot."

My mother circled, examining me.

"What are you looking for, Mom?"

"Walter," she said, "you've gotten taller and a lot more muscular."

"It must be the Vermont air," I joked, "and storing a few hundred bales in Mr. Whitcomb's hay mound."

My mother was happy to see me, but I had sensed that she was nervous from the moment I arrived. Something was wrong.

"What's going on?" I asked.

My parents glanced at each other. They were quiet. My mother sat down and looked at the floor.

Suspecting the reason for her discomfort, I finally said, "Mom, can I have the hundred and twenty dollars that I sent home? I'll go shopping this afternoon."

My mother, silent, did not look up. Instead, my father spoke: "Oh, that's gone. We needed it."

I WAS ALONE NOW. I sat on the roof of the tenement and looked up into a clear blue sky. I could hear some muffled street noises and other sounds that seemed to float up from the floors below. Earlier, I had not responded as my parents may have expected. I did not yell. I did not cry. In fact, I did not speak for several minutes, and when I did, it was only to say that I was going out.

"Are you going to see your friends now?" my mother had asked when I opened the door after quietly putting away the few clothes I had from my trip.

"Yeah, Mom, I am. I'll see you later."

I knew I wasn't ready to meet anyone from the block. So, instead, I had climbed the three flights to the roof. I wedged myself between two exhaust stacks amid a small forest of television antennas, and I cried. Small tears became wracking sobs. Then, finally, I could cry no more.

I didn't stay empty long. Anger replaced the sadness, and it filled me. I fumed. I examined my hands—scarred, calloused and hard. How many udders had they stripped? How many shovelfuls had they raised? How many bales had they hoisted? My father earned more money than anyone in the neighborhood, and my mother worked too. *Why did they take my money?*

Finally, after raging for some time to myself, my anger lost its heat. I became calm and, in a flash of cold clarity, I realized: *I am on my own.*

My parents were in debt and did not pay their bills—not because they didn't earn enough but because my father pissed away so much of it on booze. Worse, he resolved his financial problems over the years by repeatedly taking loans to pay loans—until, ultimately, the mountain was too high to scale.

My parents had built a house on sand, and the house was collapsing.

I am on my own. I absorbed the power of those words—and I felt surprisingly free: *I am on my own.*

I was sure I'd be able to find a job after school within the week. What I didn't know was that I'd soon make other choices that would change my life forever.

CHAPTER 8

I BEGAN MY junior year at A. B. Davis High School by regularly cutting classes in the morning and then working in the afternoons as a stock clerk at the Reliance Pen & Pencil factory or packing and stacking inventory for Barish's Stationery Store. After work, I generally roamed the streets with my friends.

By the middle of the school term, I was failing or barely passing most of my classes. One day, not surprisingly, a teacher advised me to switch to a vocational curriculum.

"Why?" I asked her.

"You'll never be an academic student," she explained, "and you should learn a trade so that you can earn a living."

"I'm not stupid!" I declared.

"I didn't say you were," she replied. "In fact, I think you can show how smart you are by volunteering for vocational training."

"How much do you know about me?" I demanded.

"I know your *grades*," she replied.

OFTEN, IN THE MORNINGS, instead of going to school, I'd walk over to the Mount Vernon Public Library. I was confident that I wouldn't run into any of my friends from the block—or my father—in the library, and I was sure, and correct, that it was the last place in the city that a truant officer would look for a kid playing hooky. Sometimes, late at night, I'd read one of the library books in bed by flashlight. And the more I read, the more I felt estranged from my family: *I don't belong*. I read books of every type, often guided by the advice of congenial librarians, searching for *something*.

Like so many other young readers, when I turned the pages of novels, I became the characters I found inside. I was Huck in Mark Twain's *The Adventures of Huckleberry Finn*, and I was Herbie Bookbinder in Herman Wouk's *City Boy*. Occasionally, books like John Steinbeck's *The Grapes of Wrath* and Upton Sinclair's *The Jungle* made me feel frustrated, stoking my anger as well as my conscience. Once, after I remarked to a librarian that I thought philosophy was boring and an altogether useless subject, she gave me a couple of essays by the German philosopher Arthur Schopenhauer, who spelled out a number of ways to answer the question "Who am I?" That shut me up, and I wondered, *How did she know what I was thinking?*

Books had a magic about them: I could open a page and be anywhere. I could be anyone. I could imagine myself out of a slum. When my eyes left the page, though, there was still the pain I could expect—and, of course, the fear.

One night, my father ordered me to ride with him in his car as he hunted for three men who, he said, had shown him disrespect earlier in the evening. His loaded .25 caliber pistol was on the seat between us. He warned me not to touch the weapon, then added, "Keep your goddamn eyes open and help me find the bastards."

A few blocks away, I spotted one of the men walking by himself across the street, but I stayed silent. My father saw him, though. He cursed and shouted as he raced the car over to the wrong side of the road and directly at the man, who, obviously frightened, ducked into a tenement. My father stopped the car in a screeching halt and told me to follow him. We stepped into the building's hallway, which was poorly lighted by a single hanging bulb. Fortunately, after checking every corner of the building's three urine-stenched floors, it was clear that the man had escaped.

As soon as we were back in his car, my father punched me hard in the shoulder and then hit me again. "You saw him," he said, "and don't deny it, you lying little bastard!"

I said nothing. I looked down at the seat between us for the weapon. It was gone. The pistol was in his pocket.

When we reached our apartment building, he ordered me out of the car and sped away.

I was left standing alone on the sidewalk.

"Screw you too!" I shouted angrily.

After my mother told my brother what had happened, Bill and I had the first of several discussions in which he encouraged me to enlist in the service, as he had done about a decade before. "The old man is getting worse," Bill warned me. "He beats you more than he ever beat me. He's meaner. And now that Carol is married and out of the house, you're the target. You know, he never hit Carol all that much anyway. But, like I said, you're all that's left."

A few days later, shortly after a particularly nasty confrontation of his own with our father, Bill again advised me: "You've got to get away from here and go somewhere where you can use that brain of yours." Actually, I already had been thinking about joining the military—particularly the Marines—for some time. My interest had been piqued by an experience I had in the neighborhood before I went to Vermont.

ONE NIGHT when I was fifteen, I witnessed an assault on a boy named Tony, who was two years older than I. I had known Tony from Teen Town. He was very muscular but moved—and maybe thought—a little slowly.

Tony had argued with another boy over whose turn was coming up at Ping-Pong. Actually, it was Tony's turn, and the other teenager— supported by four of his friends—was trying to cut in. Tony and the boy rushed at each other after an exchange of words at the table. One of the counselors, an adult in his forties, then stepped in and asked for identification from everyone involved, me first.

I showed him my ID card, loudly adding where I lived: *"Eleventh and Third."*

"How about *you?*" the counselor demanded, turning quickly to one of the five intruders.

"White Plains Road . . . ," the boy began, carelessly giving away that he and his four companions lived in the Wakefield section of the Bronx.

"Teen Town is for Mount Vernon residents only," the counselor said flatly. "Out. *Now!*"

With more than forty teenagers encircling the counselor—and Tony still sizzling—the five Bronx boys left amid catcalls.

Tony and I happened to leave Teen Town together a half hour later.

"Hey!" a voice shouted as we passed a corner a block away. "Wait up!"

Down the street, leaning on a black customized '49 Ford, were three of the teenagers from the Bronx, the other two sitting inside.

I felt my stomach tighten.

As the boys from the Bronx walked toward us, my pulse pounding, I noticed that the face of the tallest—the one Tony had argued with earlier—was curiously moist, glistening, as if he had oiled his skin. It made him distinctive, as did his manner, which was eerily calm.

"You want to finish it now?" he asked softly.

"Right now," Tony said, starting to slip out of his new powder-blue jacket.

The tall boy held up his hand.

"No," he said quietly, "not here. This is just between you and me—not these guys or *him*." He pointed to me, and my stomach tightened more. "Just the two of us."

On the surface, the boy from the Bronx didn't look like he could beat Tony, although he was much taller and maybe a little heavier. Tony was as strong, thick and hard-muscled as an adult construction worker. When he wore T-shirts—one sleeve rolled up with Lucky Strikes—Tony's arms, back and chest rippled. The settled confidence of the tall boy, consequently, was disconcerting.

I could see the concern deepen in Tony's eyes. Too late he realized the reality of what he was facing: His opponent had four friends with him, all but one about his own size and all his age. Tony just had me, two years younger and smaller. Plainly, we were in trouble.

The tall boy pointed toward a truck-loading platform across the street, set between two buildings. "Over there," he told Tony.

The light from the streetlamps barely reached that far back. It was dark and shadowy.

"Good," Tony replied.

Stupid, I thought.

As we crossed the street, the boy from the Bronx casually changed the rules. He pointed to the shortest guy in his group.

"You and him," he said to me.

I nodded.

Although the boy was about my height, he was at least two years older, much heavier and stronger. If I could have bolted, I would have. Instead, trying to hide my fear, I looked hard into his eyes.

To my surprise, he looked away but then turned back and whispered, "Just you and me."

His hesitancy gave me hope. *Maybe he doesn't want to fight. But if he does,* I wondered, *does he have a knife, a sharpened belt buckle?* My stomach was in a knot. Will I be stabbed or stomped? Maybe, I thought, if these guys actually let us fight one-on-one, I can hit him quickly in the nose or kick him in the groin. Who am I kidding? If I start to win, his pals will jump in. *What am I going to do?*

In my back pocket was a knife with a three-and-a-half-inch blade that sprung open from a button in the handle. I carried it only for show. I had bought it for three dollars only a few days before from another boy at Teen Town, never intending to use it. I hadn't thought I could pull a knife ever—even to keep from getting hurt. Now I wasn't sure.

Tony and the boy from the Bronx, followed by three of his friends, climbed onto the platform.

"Let's do it, man," the boy said, his hands rising to his lapels as if he were going to take off his coat.

Tony, watching him, started to shrug his own jacket from his shoulders. *No*, I thought, *don't!*

Too late.

As Tony's jacket dropped to his elbows, the other boy—his own coat still in place—slugged Tony. Quickly, one of the others squeezed Tony's jacket from behind. His large arms now bound in his own sleeves, straitjacketed, Tony cursed and struggled to free himself as the blows rained.

I froze.

The shorter boy, who had not mounted the platform with the others, glanced at me. When I didn't move, he scrambled up onto the platform to join his friends. Tony was hunched over, trying to protect himself with his back. He was too tightly centered in the group to fall as the onslaught continued.

Laughing loudly, one of the teens swung a short emergency chain, probably stolen from a subway train. Another swung a garrison belt, all as Tony screamed curses.

"What's going on over there?" a voice yelled from one of the apartments across the street. "Get out of there! I'm calling the cops!"

Still I stood entranced, unmoving, the world in slow motion.

I heard the sound of a siren.

"Let's make it!" shouted the shiny-faced boy.

All five ran past me—shoving, laughing loudly and jeering as Tony, still cursing, fell to the ground.

I turned and saw the '49 Ford pull from the curb, its tires squealing.

"It ain't done!" shouted one of the boys.

Tony, still cursing, shook his fist at them.

"How do I look?" he asked me.

Tony's left cheek was red and swollen. His lip was bleeding, and he had a bruise and a small cut on his hairline. He'd also have a black eye tomorrow. But, all things considered, he was in good shape.

"You look OK," I said. "You all right?"

"I think so," Tony told me. "I don't think nothing's broke."

"Good," I said. "Let's go back to Teen Town and get you cleaned up."

"OK," he agreed, then added angrily, "I'd like to get him back. He's yellow. I want to fight him one-on-one."

"Right," I said, though I knew that if Tony fought that boy a thousand times, he'd lose a thousand times.

Later, walking alone along Third Street, I was deep in my own thoughts and disturbed by what I perceived as my cowardice for doing nothing while Tony was being pummeled. Not far from my home, I passed the older brother of a high school classmate of mine, standing in the doorway of a poolroom. I nodded to the boy, whose nickname was Slim. He nodded back.

About half a block away—still in a cloud—I was surprised to hear someone ask, "Where you goin'?"

I looked up. The voice belonged to the shiny-faced teen from the

Bronx. Because I had been walking with my head down, distracted and deep in thought, I hadn't noticed the black '49 Ford at the curb across the street.

I realized instantly: They had heard me announce where I lived, Eleventh and Third, back in Teen Town!

"Where's your man?" the boy asked, referring to Tony.

"I don't know," I said.

"Where does he live?"

"I don't know."

Could they hear my heart? *I* could hear it. *Please,* I prayed to myself, *don't let my voice squeak.*

"I'm gonna ask you again, *four-eyes*. Where does he live?"

"Don't know," my voice cracked.

The boy from the Bronx placed his hand on my chest and pushed me back hard. I stumbled against a chain-link fence, the back of my skull cracking against the metal.

He laughed.

Cocky, toying with me as his friends giggled, he didn't notice my right hand slide into my back pocket.

I felt my neck and cheeks redden.

He put his finger on my chest.

"Where?" he asked again.

"I don't know," I repeated, this time without my voice cracking. It was as if a feather that had been tickling my stomach suddenly turned to flame. I had been humiliated. Now I was angry. The boy, backed up by four of his friends, stood against a much younger and smaller teenager: *me*. But, as had happened a few times before when my father beat me, my fear suddenly turned to white-hot rage. *I can fight through the pain,* I told myself. *Can you? I'm not Tony, and I'm not the one who's going to be suckered this time.* I knew not to show the knife: *You'll never see it coming.*

I squeezed the knife in my hand, my thumb on the button.

"I think you . . . ," the boy began, stepping toward me again. But before he could finish, he was interrupted:

"The man *said* he didn't know."

I was startled. The voice was Slim's, and the change in the air was sudden.

The boy from the Bronx had a pained expression. Behind Slim stood several of the Majestic Lords, a gang with many members on Third Street.

I had seen Slim fight only once. It was outside the poolroom with an adult, a street tough who had instigated the quarrel. Slim's younger brother Billy and I had watched him hit the man smoothly, cleanly, moving like a professional fighter. The fight had ended in less than a minute, with Slim on top. Everyone who had watched—and it was the talk of the neighborhood at the time—knew that Slim not only could box but could box well. Though Slim wasn't one of the Majestic Lords, whose members wore black-and-white sweaters, they were his friends.

Glancing around, the other four boys from the Bronx looked as uncomfortable as their shiny-faced leader, who now tried to bluff:

"This ain't your business."

"What ain't my business?" Slim asked.

"Him," he said, pointing to me. "This is between me and him."

"*Him,*" Slim said, "is my baby brother."

One of the Majestic Lords chuckled. I was very white; Slim was very black.

"He's not . . . ," but the boy stopped short of calling Slim a liar.

"Not *what?*"

The boy said nothing.

A neighborhood crowd started to form. I still held my knife tightly.

"Let's get out of here," one of the Bronx boys said.

"Get in your car," Slim ordered.

I loosened the grip on my knife.

The five started to cross the street, but Slim stopped the boy with the shiny face. "Not *you*," he said. "You got to pay a toll." Then Slim slapped the boy.

It was so sudden, no one—least of all the boy from the Bronx—expected it.

The boy glowered. "I don't want no trouble," he said, turning away.

Then, spinning quickly, he tried to land a punch. But Slim stepped to the side, and the boy missed completely, stumbling and twisting sideways.

Slim slapped him again.

"Don't come back," Slim said, faking another slap. When the boy raised his hands, falling for the feint, Slim punched him in the stomach.

"Hear me?" Slim asked.

The boy, gasping, nodded.

"Take him home," Slim told the others, none of whom had moved since the first slap.

Amid catcalls and challenges from the Majestic Lords, the five quietly got into their car. Then, after the car had driven a safe distance, it stopped briefly, and the five shouted curses.

Several people on the street burst into laughter as the car sped off. Then the crowd dispersed, leaving Slim and me. Still shaken, I thanked him.

"Next month," he told me, "you won't have me around to get you and Billy out of trouble."

"Where are you going?"

"The Marines."

"That's great," I said. "Billy told me you were going to enlist, Slim. Hey, good luck!"

"Now take off," he told me, laughing, "before *Mom* gets worried."

Alone in bed an hour later, I trembled, aware of just how close I had come to stabbing the kid from the Bronx. I would have been caught by the cops, I realized, and I almost certainly would be in jail now, instead of lying here under a blanket. *I'm no different from the old man!*

But as soon as I thought that, I knew it wasn't true. I *am* different. Bill is right: I don't belong here! Once again I swore to myself: *I have to get out.*

To my surprise, the following afternoon, when I told Tony what had happened, he was more impressed with Slim going into the Marines than he was with the fight.

"I'm going to be a Marine too!" he declared.

"You are?"

"Yeah."

"Why?" I asked.

"They're the baddest," he told me, adding somberly, "and everybody respects 'em!"

"Really?"

"Man," he said, "Parris Island boot camp is bad news—but I'll make it. I do a lot of push-ups. Yeah, I'm going in the Marines too."

ROSEMARY AND I were both sixteen—thankfully, I was some months older—and she was popular among our friends. To my mind, Rosemary was quite beautiful. I, in contrast, felt like a toad. I hated my eyeglasses, could never seem to comb my hair right, and I knew with precision the location of every pimple on my forehead. Inside, I smoldered with self-doubt. I tried to hide my insecurity behind a swagger, but a small balloon seemed to swell in my stomach whenever I'd think of Rosemary.

Arriving for a date with Rosemary one Saturday night, I grunted my way through saying hello to her parents. Then, despite my tongue-tied replies, we somehow made it through the front door.

"Your parents are nice," I said. *Dumb*, I thought. *What a dumb thing to say.*

"Thank you," she replied, laughing. "I kind of like them."

Maybe that wasn't so dumb after all.

"Yeah," I added, "they're *really* nice."

She laughed again.

My brain cells had emptied—I had no thoughts. I could *feel* the silence. *Say something,* I told myself. I felt the balloon swell larger in my stomach. Say *something!*

"I'm going to be a Marine!" I declared.

"You *are?*" she replied.

Was that respect I heard in Rosemary's voice?

"I think they have the best uniforms," she said.

It *was* respect.

"I'll get my uniform right away," I told her, without the slightest clue as to whether that was true.

Quietly, my brother Bill had continued to encourage me to enlist in the service, and joining the Marines had crossed my mind several times since Slim had enlisted the year before. Even Tony's wild claim struck a chord inside me: "They're the baddest, and everybody respects 'em!" Tony, though—muscles and all—had been turned down by the Marines, and he never told anyone why. Now my declaration to Rosemary was causing me to face up to what I really feared: *Would the Marines reject me too?*

Rosemary and I had fun that night. On the way home, we chattered about the movie we'd seen, not the Marines. Then, after an awkward but pleasant moment at her door, I announced: "I'm going to talk to the recruiter in New Rochelle on Monday, after school." And I kept my word.

"WALTER, WHY DO YOU want to drop out of high school?" asked Maurice Childs, the vice principal of A. B. Davis High School.

Because, I said to myself, *I want to escape.* The tension between my

father and me had never been more volatile or more violent. The beatings were escalating. Worse, I was becoming almost as angry as my
father—and, indulging my emerging temper, I was quick to fight
almost anyone over the smallest slight. I stayed on the street as much as
possible, mainly walking and talking the nights away with my friends.
Inevitably, though, I would return home—to silence or to rage. I could
not be sure, ever, what awaited me behind that apartment door.

Quitting school to join the Marines was my way out. My brother,
who understood that one way or another I was going to leave home,
had helped my mother persuade my father to sign the enlistment papers
so that I could go to Parris Island the week following my seventeenth
birthday.

"I'm failing every subject except English," I told Mr. Childs. "I have
enough cut slips to serve detentions for twenty years, and I'm tired of
people messing with me."

Mr. Childs, a gentle, white-haired man, reminded me that two years
earlier I had been an honors student at Windward who had been
skipped from the eighth to the tenth grade. "Walter," he said, "I cannot
stop you, but I want to know why you're doing so poorly."

"There's nothing to know," I replied, aware that he had guessed I
was intentionally failing my courses. "I don't want to stay in school," I
said. "That's all." *Would you like to know,* I thought, *why sometimes I feel
safer on a street corner than in my own bed?*

"You're only sixteen. What do you plan to do?" he asked.

"I am going to be a Marine."

"Don't you think," he asked, "that the Marines might 'mess with
you' even more than your teachers?"

"You don't understand, Mr. Childs," I said.

He reached across his desk and squeezed my hand.

"Good luck," he said.

CHAPTER 9

I T WAS FIVE-THIRTY on the morning of September 6, 1961. I
stepped out of the doorway of 159 South Eleventh Avenue and
took a deep breath. The block was quiet. I walked slowly across the
street, paused, turned back and looked up toward the second floor. My
mother, who was holding the blinds to one side, smiled and waved to me.

I waved back and started up Third Street toward the Bronx. After a
few steps, I stopped again to look back. The window was empty. Years
later, I would learn that my mother had stayed at the window but had
not wanted me to remember seeing her cry. She had hid behind the
blinds and watched me until I was out of sight. My seventeenth birthday had been only six days before. It had been almost three years since
the night when I'd washed someone else's blood from my face, sat
alone on a stoop and first promised myself in the darkness: *I'm getting
out of here*. I strode past the telephone booth where I'd found that blood

and, almost involuntarily, raised my hand to check my face. I laughed. *Not anymore*, I thought. I was on my way. And although I hadn't slept well and it was early in the day, I was exhilarated.

As I walked toward the subway at 241st Street and White Plains Road to start the hour ride to 39 Whitehall Street in lower Manhattan, my excitement dimmed and the butterflies started in my stomach. I thought about a movie called *Marines, Let's Go*, which I had watched a few nights earlier. I had noticed, painfully, that everyone in it looked old enough to be my father.

I wondered if anyone at Parris Island, South Carolina, would be near my age. *What if I don't make it?* I worried. I remember the next few hours only through the haze of too many years.

At 39 Whitehall Street, I was placed in a squad with about a half-dozen other Marine recruits from the New York area. To my relief, all were about my age. Our squad was to take a train to Yemassee, South Carolina, which would be the last stop before we reached Parris Island. Because we were lined up alphabetically, I was given everyone's orders by a corporal and told to present them to a Marine who would be waiting for us at Yemassee.

"Don't lose 'em, boy!" the corporal warned me. "Your drill instructor won't like that." He chuckled.

Our nervous squad changed trains in Washington, D.C., after a considerable delay. A much larger group, composed of troops from throughout Pennsylvania, joined us. Day had become night, but no one really slept, although everyone pretended to be asleep.

Shortly after dawn, the train arrived at Yemassee. I saw a Marine on the platform. He was tall and thin, and I noticed that he was a sergeant. Wanting to be helpful and to be rid of the orders I carried, I hailed him: "Hey, Mac, these for you?"

Thus began my first lesson as a Marine: A recruit does not call a sergeant "Mac." A recruit does not call a sergeant *at all*. The sergeant explained this to me and the other recruits very quickly.

"Boy!" he began, his mouth only an inch from my face but his voice loud enough to be heard fifty yards away. "I am a sergeant! You are a turd! Understand me, boy?"

"Yes," I said, my voice ready to crack.

"Yes, *what*?" he demanded.

"Yes, *sir*!" I shouted.

"How come I only hear one boy?"

Every recruit bellowed, "Yes, *sir*!"

"I can't hear you, *girls*!"

"Yes, sir!" we shouted in unison.

The next few hours were a blur of angry voices, uncertainty, running, falling and rushing. We passed through Recruit Receiving, packaged and mailed our civilian clothes home, were issued a green "utility outfit" and black boots, had our heads shaved and were assigned to a platoon. Then we met our drill instructors, Staff Sergeant Sawchik and his assistant, Sergeant McCall, two lanky and unsmiling men who were wearing Smokey the Bear hats pinned with the Marine emblem.

"When you were home, your momma took care of you," Staff Sergeant Sawchik told us. "Now you're mine. I'm not your momma. I'm not your friend. But I'm all you got. Welcome to Parris Island, girls!"

"Yes, sir!" shouted Platoon 166, First Battalion.

"I can't hear you, girls," he said softly.

"Yes, *sir*!" we tried, our voices cracking.

"Down for push-ups!" he ordered, and down we went.

After lights-out that night, our barracks sounded like a pneumonia ward. Everybody seemed to have the sniffles, including me.

What have I done? I asked myself, convinced that I'd never survive Sawchik and McCall.

≈

ONE MORNING, after the last recruit in our platoon had been issued an M1 rifle, Sergeant McCall sat us down in a circle. As each of us tightly clutched his new weapon, the sergeant began to read from the Creed of the United States Marines: "This is my rifle. There are many like it, but this one is mine. My rifle is my best friend. It is my life. I must master it as I must master my life . . ." He spoke slowly as he continued to read, pausing about midway through to emphasize two sentences: "My rifle and myself know that what counts in war is not the rounds we fire, the noise of our burst, nor the smoke we make. We know that it is the hits that count."

We know that it is the hits that count. The drill instructors stressed results in all endeavors, not just learning how to accurately fire a weapon. Again and again in the days and weeks that followed, the drill instructors hammered the point that Marines regard each other solely by performance. Only once did I hear good intentions praised.

One recruit had struggled harder than the rest of us to learn the Manual of Arms, which is basically the movements made when drilling or standing with a rifle. In nearly every maneuver in close-order drill, this recruit became confused. Every night after lights-out, though, he practiced. One of us invariably volunteered to work with him, but he'd almost always outlast us and continue to practice for hours after everyone else was asleep. Without fail, though, he'd foul up again the following day. He had the same problem with General Orders, the standard rules of behavior that each of us had to memorize from the Marine guidebook. He couldn't seem to get them in the right order, no matter how hard he tried.

One afternoon, the recruit was told to report to the drill instructor. He did not return. Later that night, Staff Sergeant Sawchik told us we would not see that recruit again. He was going to be discharged from the Marine Corps—*honorably*, the drill instructor said, adding: "He has as much guts as any Marine I've known. We had to make the decision *for* him. He did not quit."

I vowed that I would not quit either.

SLOWLY, DAY BY DAY, we started to become a team. We came to depend on each other, to help each other under the most difficult circumstances. We learned killing techniques—but we also learned how to lift and carry a fellow Marine and his rifle to safety in combat. Gradually, the cloud of confusion began to evaporate. The language had meaning: A "bulkhead" was a wall, a "deck" was the floor, a "rack" was a bed, a "head" was a bathroom, a "hatch" was a door. Even the pile of "782 Gear"—a polyglot assortment of items from a canteen cup to a knapsack to tents and poles—began to make sense.

Each night, the drill instructors also discussed everything from hygiene to moral principles, emphasizing qualities such as integrity and courage. As teachers, the two men were unambiguous. Sergeant McCall, for example, clarified race relations for us simply: "All Marines are the same color—*green*. And don't forget it." The drill instructors also explained that a recruit, according to his own faith, could attend services and receive instruction from a Roman Catholic, Protestant or Jewish chaplain. Or not at all.

Finally, I *belonged*.

IT WAS 2200—10:00 P.M.—on November 22, 1961, a cool evening, and I looked into the darkness, smiling. I'd made it! The joy was palpable in the silence. Each recruit felt it. The next morning, we were scheduled to board buses to leave Parris Island for Camp Lejeune in North Carolina for advanced infantry training. *We* had made it! Of the original seventy-five, eight had dropped out and four were added along the way. Platoon 166 numbered seventy-one Marines.

"I know you're awake," Staff Sergeant Sawchik's voice rasped and echoed through the barracks, "so listen up."

What now? I worried.

"I'd be proud to lead this platoon anywhere. Never conduct yourselves less than the best, because you are the best. You are United States Marines."

He paused, then added, "Good night, *men*."

The barracks exploded into a uniform shout: "Good night, *sir*!"

For the second time in boot camp, my eyes filled.

CHAPTER 10

Traces of moonlight flickered across the silent, orderly rows of dark-green blankets, each one wrapped around a sleeping body. I studied one slight, moving beam and watched it scatter faintly across a wall—no, a "bulkhead." I followed it to the ceiling—no, the "overhead." Enough!

I was seventeen, a Marine private first class stationed at Camp Lejeune, North Carolina. Again I studied my watch: 0200.

Why can't I sleep? What's troubling me? Hidden behind the thickening clouds that crowded my mind was an idea—maybe a problem—and I couldn't reach it, couldn't quite touch it.

Resigned to a sleepless night, I slid quietly out of my rack, slipped on my green utility trousers and my green utility jacket, laced my black boots, donned my green hat, stepped through the hatch and lit a Pall Mall. I had enlisted only seven months earlier, but

I felt like I had been in the Marine Corps all my life. Did I dream the rest?

In boot camp, I had felt elated because I finally belonged somewhere. Now, despite the camaraderie in the Corps, I was feeling confused. *Do I have a home somewhere?* I wondered. *Am I ever getting out?* That's it! Am I ever getting out?

During the previous few weeks, I'd endured the endless banter of two "short-timers" in my outfit—Marines about to be released after completing their four-year enlistments.

"How short are you?" one would say.

"I'm so short, I've got to look up to look down," the other would reply.

"Can someone help me with my socks?"

"Why?"

"I'm too short. Can't reach 'em."

I, on the other hand, was a new Marine, a "boot," so I would be teased: "Anderson, tell me again, how long *you* got?"

"Three years and five months," I'd respond wearily.

"Three years! And what?" would come the retort. "I don't even have time to say it! I'm too short."

Those three years could just as easily have been three *hundred* years. For me, it seemed an eternity. Adding to my dismay, I no longer felt at home in the civilian world.

Three months earlier, I had returned to Mount Vernon on leave after about a hundred days of boot camp at Parris Island and advanced infantry training at Camp Lejeune, and I had been struck by the complete shift in my perception.

I now saw litter. In the Marines, even cigarettes were "field-stripped" down to the tobacco and paper after they were smoked. Along Third Street, I eyeballed cigarette butts, patches of lint and dirt, candy wrappers and beer cans strewn about. Riding the subway from Manhattan to 241st Street, I had remained standing, not wanting to crease or soil my trousers. In my neighborhood, most of the pants I saw needed cleaning and pressing.

But I also saw colors. Having lived from dawn to dark immersed in Marine green during my first few months of training, I found a spectacular rainbow amid the streets of Mount Vernon and its lights, the parked cars, the disordered rows of houses and office buildings, the billboards and the clothes the civilians wore.

WHERE DO I BELONG? I wondered. *There or here? Will I ever get out?*

That's *not* why I can't sleep, I now realized. Involuntarily, I breathed deeply. It was coming to me.

I will get out of the Marines one day.

The words flashed like neon, bursting a dam and flooding me with unbalanced, conflicting thoughts.

But what will I do then?

Shaken, I returned to my rack, undressed silently, crawled under the blanket and lay my head on the pillow, my eyes wide.

I have to be a man. I have to make plans for my future, get an education. In three years and five months—suddenly, it didn't seem so long!—I'll be a civilian, on my own. I'll be twenty-one. I'll be a man. There's no escape. I can't be a kid anymore.

Twenty-one? It seemed old.

A few hours later, in the daylight, I asked to see the first sergeant.

"What's up?" he asked.

"I want to go to school," I said.

THIS, I KNEW, was only a drill; clearly, I had no chance. It was June 1963, and I was seventh in line to be interviewed for promotion to lance corporal.

"What are we supposed to do?" I asked the Marine standing behind me.

"Go through the motions," he suggested. "Where you and I are standing, the only thing we're going to make today is liberty—if we're lucky."

"Right," I agreed. "Maybe they'll get this over fast, so we can change clothes and go to town."

"Now, that's a *good* idea," he said, "because this stuff means nothing to me."

"Me neither," I lied.

The truth was, I *wanted* to be promoted. In a few days, I'd be graduating from the last of the three electronics courses I had attended for almost a year. Unfortunately, the training, however useful, kept me off promotion lists: No Marine could be promoted while still a student. I had become a private first class with twenty-one months in the Marine Corps. I also had passed high school and one-year college equivalency exams. For motivation when the studying had been most difficult, I had told myself that at least I was learning how to be a better-educated PFC.

Occasionally, though, my frustration led me to lose my temper during those long months of study. While others got promoted and were able to give orders, I still had to take them: *You, the Marine with all the schooling—sweep up the barracks.*

I knew my education was worth more than that, but, after almost two years, I was eager to be promoted. Not that I wasn't proud of what I had achieved. I knew that five times I had faced a challenge in the Marines, the most significant being the first: surviving and then graduating from Parris Island boot camp. Completing advanced infantry training without a hitch also had given me confidence. Now, completing academics in these technical schools—particularly the math portion, since I had failed algebra in high school—had me looking at myself differently. I remembered the day I had walked into the San Diego Marine

Corps Recruit Depot, where the electronics school battalion was located, worried whether I could pass. Meeting my classmates didn't help. Many had attended or graduated from college; I was the only high school dropout.

Convinced that the Marine Corps had made a terrible mistake—I was not prepared for this!—I sat on my footlocker and stewed. But then, after a few minutes, I could almost hear the person who had so believed in me: "Walter, you can do this," Mrs. Williams had said. And I prayed, "Let me just pass one course."

Fortunately, the school assumed (correctly, in my case) that we knew *nothing*. We were taught everything we needed to know, from the most basic math to the more complex formulas necessary for understanding electronics. I persevered and finished eleventh in a class of twenty in my first course, eighth of seventeen in the second course, and seventh of twenty-four in the third course. Originally, I had hoped to pass, period. But at some point I began to want to do more than get by; I wanted to do *well*. Students in the top third in our final course, I learned, would be interviewed for promotion, and three actually would be promoted.

As I stood on line as the seventh out of the eight candidates, I thought: *Well, I did my best, and if that's not good enough.* . . . No, it's *not* good enough, I admitted to myself. Private First Class Anderson, you're not going to be promoted today—not Number Seven.

"What did they ask?" I queried Number Five as he strode out.

"The lifer question," he said. " 'Are you going to stay in the Marine Corps?'"

"What did you tell them?"

He laughed loudly.

After Number Six, I was ordered into a small office to be interviewed by a captain, a second lieutenant and a first sergeant.

The captain spoke first: "Why are you here?"

"Sir," I said, "to be considered for promotion to lance corporal."

"Should you be promoted?"

"Yes, sir."

The captain glanced past the second lieutenant to the first sergeant.

"Why should we promote you," the sergeant asked, "when we can promote One, Two and Three?"

"I can't speak for them, first sergeant, only for me."

"Why *you*, then?"

"About a year and a half ago, I was a high school dropout," I said. "Today I have a high school GED, a one-year college GED, and I have successfully graduated from three communications courses. I have proved myself."

The lieutenant interrupted: "What if you're *not* promoted?"

"I still have proved myself," I said, and I knew it was true. I *had* proved myself. Suddenly, it was as if a heavy seabag had been lifted from my shoulders. I was no longer nervous. Now I was going to enjoy this interview.

"Are you going to stay in the Marine Corps?" the lieutenant asked.

The "lifer question"! *Aha*, I thought. *I have to take a risk.*

"Sir," I said, "I have more than two years to go. Would you believe me if I told you I was going to stay in?"

"Would *you* believe you?" the lieutenant asked.

"No," I said, "I would not. And something else . . ."

"What's that?"

"I don't plan to stay in. And that's the truth. I have every intention of getting out of the Marine Corps, *sir*."

The captain and the first sergeant dropped their heads, almost simultaneously. *Did they smile?* I wondered.

The lieutenant, who seemed annoyed with me, asked: "Are you going to continue your education?"

"Yes, sir."

"Why?"

"Frankly, sir, after completing these courses, I think I can continue—and I'm going to."

"Do you know what you want to be?"

I paused.

"No, sir," I said. "I do not." I *was* enjoying myself, standing there and telling the truth. The risk had been worth it, whether I was promoted or not.

"Any idea?" the lieutenant pressed.

"I'm not sure," I said. "Sometimes I dream about writing, but I don't have the education. I'm going to give what I've learned here a good shot. Then I'll see."

"Anderson," said the captain, who had been silent, "you're very proud of yourself, aren't you?"

"Yes, sir, I am."

"And you don't expect to be promoted, do you?"

"No, sir."

"Good guess," the lieutenant blurted.

I thought I saw the captain's eyes flicker, but he continued as if the lieutenant had not spoken.

"Son," he said, "I know you're telling the truth. I hope, though, that you're telling it for the right reasons and not simply because you don't think you can be promoted anyway." He paused. "Let me tell you some of what your instructors say about you: You had the least education of any student in your class, and you should have finished last. Finishing seventh means you studied your butt off."

I listened silently, enjoying the report.

"And they also say you have trouble controlling your temper. Is that true?"

"No, sir," I replied, a little too quickly.

The captain arched an eyebrow.

The lieutenant smiled. He and I were destined to dislike each other intensely; at least I was sure *I* disliked *him*.

"Are you certain?" asked the first sergeant, his face serious.

"Sir, I'm determined—no, *enthusiastic*," I added, searching for a word. "Look, I have a temper, but I do control it. You don't know how hard I work to keep my temper . . ."

The captain interrupted. "What would you like to say to the lieutenant here?"

The lieutenant looked perplexed.

I paused.

"I don't believe we think much of each other, sir."

"Anderson, that's not what I asked you."

"I have nothing to say to the lieutenant," I replied evenly, and that was true.

"If you're promoted to lance corporal," the first sergeant said, "the next step is corporal, then maybe even sergeant—a noncommissioned officer. Are you ready to be an NCO?"

"Yes, sir, I am."

"Would you be a *good* NCO?" the lieutenant asked.

"Yes, sir," I said, expecting that I wouldn't have the opportunity this time around regardless.

"Dismissed," the first sergeant said.

"How was it?" Number Eight asked as I walked past him.

"Not bad," I said, "but watch out for the lieutenant."

"Did you make it?" he asked. "Are you going to be promoted?"

"You've got to be kidding," I said, laughing loudly. "Not today."

Two hours later, I got a call from a Marine named Linda whom I had dated and who worked in the office. "Andy," she confided, "you're a lance corporal!"

"Me?"

"No kidding!" she insisted. "I've got their notes right here. All three put you right on top."

"Even the lieutenant?"

"Andy," she said, confused by my question, "*he* recommended you."

⁓

I COULD FEEL the moisture beading on the back of my neck as I stood at attention under the warm midday sun with more than a hundred other Marines a few yards from our barracks at Camp Pendleton in California. *Why*, I wondered, *had we been ordered to formation so unexpectedly?* Our executive officer—a tall, lean captain—emerged from one of the offices, walked briskly toward the assembled men, stopped, turned stiffly and faced us.

"I need volunteers . . . ," he began, and I silently groaned to myself. *Not this time*, I vowed. It was 1965, and I was a twenty-year-old corporal with only a few months left to serve on active duty.

"For duty in Southeast Asia," he continued. "Not all of you will be assigned," he said. "Some will stay back at Pendleton. Volunteers, take one step forward."

It must be chilly in New York this time of year, I told myself, but it will be steaming hot in Vietnam. No reason to volunteer. None of that gung-ho stuff for me. I should play it safe. I'm a short-timer. Let someone else step forward this time. Why do they have to ask me *now?* Most of these guys won't volunteer anyway, not the Marines I serve with—not these, the world's greatest gripers. Well, some of them might, but I'll bet half don't.

Knock it off, Anderson. Are you going with them or not? I asked myself. If *I* volunteer, those who don't will tease me unmercifully. I took a deep breath. *I don't believe what I'm about to do. I know I'm going to make a mistake.* My jaw tightened. I stepped forward.

"At ease!" the captain ordered, and for at least half a minute he was silent.

A single laugh erupted, followed by another and then another, until everyone, even the captain, was laughing. I looked to my left, then to my right. Each man had assessed the risk and had drawn his own conclusion. And every Marine in that formation at Camp Pendleton, officer and enlisted man alike, had volunteered for Vietnam.

IT WAS ABOUT 2100—9:00 P.M.—and I sat on the deck of the troop ship with a buddy, Tom Satterlee, as it sliced through the sea on its way to Vietnam. I had scoured the ship's small library early that morning, looking for a thin volume—something I could read quickly. I had picked a book called *Night* by an author I did not recognize, Elie Wiesel. Then I'd found a comfortable spot on the ship's deck where I wouldn't be disturbed, plopped down and begun to read. Soon I had become engrossed. *Night* was gripping and raw—an account of the Nazi death camps as seen through the eyes of a young Jewish boy whose family was destroyed and whose faith in God was challenged.

I was shaken and wanted to talk with someone about what I'd read. Tom, though, had not read *Night*. So, after I'd prattled on for a while, we changed the subject to the most common topic among our fellow Marines: *getting out.*

"Andy," Tom asked, "are you going back home when you get out?"

"No," I said, "I'm going to live in California. I'll find a job and go to college. I think I can go to school free after a year."

"You're not going home at all?"

"Just a visit. When they let me out of the Marine Corps, I'll visit my family for a few days, then go back to California for good."

Tom was even-tempered like my boyhood pal Barry Williams, and smart. We confided in each other. I knew for some time how badly he wanted to be a pilot, and I was sure he'd find a way to make it to flight school. And Tom knew why my stay in New York would be short.

"You hate him, don't you?" he asked. Tom didn't need to identify "him."

"Tom," I said, "if my father ever tries to hit me again, I'll take him out. So I can't be around him."

Tom didn't reply. Other than the splashing sound the ship made each time its bow dipped into the ocean, the evening was nearly silent. Down below deck, most of the Marines and sailors were either watching a movie in the mess, playing cards, sleeping or gabbing. Above, the night sky seemed almost as white as it was black—awash with blazing stars, one brighter than the next.

After a while, Tom ended the soothing silence. "Andy," he said, "I'd like to ask you something about your father, but I don't want you to get pissed off."

I laughed and encouraged him: "Tommy, I don't think there's a question I haven't thought of when it comes to the old man. Go ahead."

"Are you sure he's your father?" Tom asked.

I had asked myself that question many times, but I always dismissed it: Wishing that my father wasn't my father wouldn't make it so. No one else had ever asked me, though. I wasn't angry; I was curious.

"Why do you ask?"

"You don't look like your brother or your sister in your snapshots. I think both of them look like your father. I'll bet you *think* differently too. But the real thing is the beatings. Hell, I don't know . . ."

"Tom," I said, "I've thought about it a lot. And, believe me, I'd be happier if he *wasn't* my father. But that would mean my mom slept with another guy. I can't picture that. Also, she can't keep a secret to save her life. I would *know*."

"Maybe you do, pal."

CHAPTER 11

HERE ARE SOME papers for you!" the PFC shouted as he lifted a tightly wrapped bundle of *Stars and Stripes* across his lap and tossed it out of the window of his truck. The newspapers landed softly in the sand a few feet away.

"How bad was it last night?" he asked. His voice was excited—too excited to suit me.

"Move it!" rasped the unshaven staff sergeant near me, his voice and patience worn reed-thin after the sleepless night we had shared.

It was hot. I was moist and sticky, and my undershirt and trousers felt heavy and wet. It was 0900 on October 27, 1965, at a helicopter landing strip in East Da Nang, in the Republic of Vietnam. The China Sea was only a few feet away, and nearby Marble Mountain seemed to rise out of the sand like a foreboding mound of charcoal. A few hours earlier—four minutes after midnight, by my watch—this camp and its few hundred servicemen had come under a surprise attack by the Viet Cong. The thunderous assault had instantly awakened everyone, including me. Several helicopters had been lost in brilliant, searing explosions.

The enemy's dead and wounded had been taken to the center of our camp in the darkness. The prisoners were questioned in one area, and the dead were placed side by side on the ground in another.

One dead attacker, I noticed, was much smaller than the others. I placed my foot under his chest and lifted, turning him over. He had been a child, no more than ten years old, and his remains lay sand-wiched amid those of twelve other broken bodies. None of them looked real to me except this one boy. His eyes were open, and his face was expressionless. His death must have been a surprise, I reasoned, because neither pain nor fear had been frozen into his features. Curious, I thought, how the others—all adults, some with limbs missing, their blood imperceptible in the shadows—looked like waxen mannequins. I felt nothing for them. Yet the boy touched me.

"Andy," a lieutenant called out, "what's the matter?"

"Look at this," I answered, pointing to the boy.

"Damn!" he exclaimed. "It's just a kid."

"Yeah," I said, "a kid."

"Let's go," he ordered.

I nodded.

We had walked only a few feet when a dead Marine was carried past us on a stretcher. He was about my height and weight, and he was prob-ably young—but I could not be sure, because most of his skull was missing. My jaw tightened and my face reddened. My compassion for that little Viet Cong soldier instantly turned to disgust. Now only the Marine mattered to me.

I had been trained to be a Marine, to follow and to lead Marines, to understand that my life depended on them, their courage, their tenacity, their honor. I knew that no matter how loudly or frequently we griped— and we complained often and mightily—finally, despite every difference we carried with us into the Corps, it was only each other that we could trust. I could depend on them; they could depend on me. Hurt them, and you hurt me. The dead Marine was one of us, and his death hurt.

Now, hours later, the sun was bright and the cleanup already had begun.

"Hey, Andy," a lance corporal called to me, "look at this crap!"

He handed me a copy of *Stars and Stripes* from the bundle the PFC had tossed to us. I read the story that had angered him, a report of an anti-Vietnam demonstration.

I stood.

"Where are you going?" a staff sergeant asked.

"I'm going to see if I can find a typewriter," I replied.

"In that mess?"

A few yards away was another unit's headquarters tent that had become a casualty of the night, its chairs overturned and its cardboard file boxes, reports, orders and paper folders in disarray. I lifted and probed and finally found a sticky but serviceable manual typewriter.

I set a cardboard carton holding C rations firmly in the sand, placed the typewriter on top of it and inserted a sheet of paper I had found. Then I sat on a small stool and, with the sun burning into my neck and back, I typed:

> *Just what is Vietnam?*
>
> *It is a most beautiful 16-year-old girl, who fluently speaks three languages . . . an elderly man who can barely speak his own village dialect. It is a Montagnard chieftain sawing out a girl's teeth as she reaches the "age of wisdom" . . . she sheds not a tear. It is a cocktail party in Saigon . . . a raiding party in Plei Me.*
>
> *It is an orphanage in Da Nang with a Marine "adopting" a small child for the day . . . that Marine in a foxhole at night. It is fear . . . and humor as only servicemen accomplish. It is receiving let-*

ters from home . . . and no mail. It is our paper . . . the Stars and Stripes.

It is heat, dust, sand . . . and it is monsoon. It is jungle . . . and mountain range. It is insects . . . and malaria pills. It is never-ending shots from the "Doc" . . . It is shots from V.C. It is a people fighting for their freedom . . . and those against it.

It is Charlie, who believes he is "liberating" the Vietnamese peasants . . . It is Charlie defecting when he learns he was duped. It is the sorrowful experience of reading about an anti-U.S. Vietnam demonstration.

It is pride when reading of Congressmen and college students giving blood. It is hate . . . and it is love. It is boys becoming men . . . and it is men dying. It is a sense of knowledge . . . and doing what is really right by God and country. It is cleaning a rifle . . . and firing a rifle. It is a rich American . . . and a poor child.

It is rice paddies . . . and it is Xichlo (cyclo) cabs. It is sampans . . . and it is the U.S.S. Coral Sea. *It is Military Pay Currency, "funny money" . . . and it is piasters. It is an ARVN friend . . . and a Viet Cong prisoner. It is an order obeyed . . . and a mission accomplished. It is aiding a villager . . . and curing the sick . . . helping the needy help themselves. It is a chaplain at Chu Lai . . . It is the .45 on his hip.*

Above and beyond all else . . . it is Americans helping a people remain free . . . not by blood alone but by the more important concern, realization of human compassion. It is, by the alertness and courage of our country, accomplishment! As God will judge, we are right!

I had paused for a few seconds each time I mentioned God. It didn't seem quite right bringing God into the war—and, considering my own religious experience so far, I wasn't sure how God would judge anything. But, finally, I decided the allusion was my way of emphasizing that I thought our work here was important. Only when I had finished typing did I become aware that the staff sergeant and the lance corporal stood side by side behind me, reading over my shoulder.

"That's *something*," the staff sergeant said.

"What are you going to do with it?" the lance corporal asked.

"I don't know," I said, "maybe send it home."

AFTER IT HAD remained folded in my pocket for a couple of days, I finally decided to mail what I had typed to my hometown newspaper, the *Daily Argus* in Mount Vernon, as a letter to the editor. I posted the letter, then forgot about it.

A few weeks later, our platoon commander, Lieutenant Brian Gillian, phoned from Da Nang and told me that I had been promoted to sergeant. "Hop a ride to mainside," he suggested, "so the company commander can make this official and the rest of us can congratulate you."

"Yes, sir," I said, acutely aware that it had to be the lieutenant himself who had recommended the promotion. It was unusual. I was twenty-one, and although I already had served almost three months longer than my original four-year enlistment because of various extensions, I had made it clear that I was not going to be a career Marine. In four months I would be released from active duty—a civilian again—and, as anyone within earshot of me could have confirmed, I was counting the days.

"Why did you promote me?" I asked the lieutenant when I arrived to receive my new stripes.

"Because," he said, "in case you haven't noticed, you're in the Marine Corps. No one here cares whether you're a short-timer or a lifer. Anyway, there might not be 'four months from now' for anyone. We want the best people in charge day to day. We'll worry about 'four months' in four months. Congratulations!"

He put out his hand. I shook it and said, "Thank you, sir."

"Are you going right back to the airstrip?" he asked.

"I'm going to pick up the mail for our guys," I said, "then I'll hitch a ride. I'll celebrate this promotion when we get back to California."

"I'll bet you will," he said, laughing.

When I signed for the mail, I was handed a canvas pouch with about forty letters and discovered, to my astonishment, that more than thirty were addressed to me. The editor of the *Daily Argus* had published what I had written that October morning in East Da Nang—not on the letters page but on the front page on November 20, 1965. Copies were enclosed with several of the letters. A boot-camp picture of me in a dress-blue uniform appeared with the article, and I noticed immediately that I was identified as a corporal. The page was packed with Vietnam stories: "South Viets Join Battle," "U.S. Cavalrymen Given Help in Ia Drang area," "California Police Ready for Viet Peace Marchers," "North Viet Troops Seen Matching U.S. Buildup," "A Suggestion: Draft Cards of Aluminum," "Communist Party Plans to Appeal Conviction for Not Registering." And—flush in the middle—was my picture with the headline "Just What Is Vietnam? City Marine Tells Us."

A letter from my mother began, "Daddy and I are very proud of you."

CHAPTER 12

THE BUILDING AT 673 Locust Street was an apartment house in the Fleetwood section of Mount Vernon, only a few blocks from Immanuel Lutheran School. It was where my parents had moved after my father retired from Con Edison in his mid-fifties, while I was in Vietnam.

"It even has an elevator," my father told me when I arrived on leave shortly before Christmas in 1965. "But," he added, "that don't mean nothing to me." Such comments, I knew, were storm warnings. Trouble was brewing in my father's mind. He padded off to the kitchen while I dropped my seabag in the living room and began to unpack.

I was weary, and the last thing I wanted was an argument. *This stay*, I thought to myself, *is going to be short*. A group of us had been flown from Vietnam to Okinawa, where we stayed one raucous night; then we flew directly to El Toro, California, where we received our orders. I was assigned to the San Diego Marine Corps Recruit Depot but was given a fifteen-day leave before reporting. I now wondered whether I'd wasted the few dollars I had by flying to New York.

"Vietnam ain't nothing," my father started ranting from the kitchen. "The Marines neither! Just like your brother, with his 'police action.' Korea was no war!"

Sitting in the living room with my mother, I told her: "Mom, I love you, but I can't stay."

"I don't want you to leave," she said, "but I understand. Sometimes I think it gets better, then . . ."

"I know you're talking in there!" my father shouted, and I heard a chair scrape the linoleum floor of the kitchen. Looking up as I began repacking my seabag, I saw my father standing in the hallway between the two rooms. His neck and face had reddened, and his eyes were narrowed. "You're going nowhere!" he challenged, his voice hard and angry.

I closed the seabag and laid it aside as I slipped on my Marine jacket, then stepped toward my father.

"Where do you think *you're* going?" he demanded.

"I'm leaving."

"No, you're not!"

"Take a good look at me," I said, my voice harsh. "I'm not the kid you used to beat up."

"What do you think you're going to do?" he taunted.

"Please stop it," my mother pleaded. "Let him go!"

At six feet, I was two inches taller than my father, thirty-five years younger and at least twenty-five pounds heavier, though I had only a thirty-two-inch waist.

"Look at me!" I ordered.

He looked directly into my eyes.

"What do you see?" I asked.

"Nothing much," he said. "Nothing I can't handle."

It was as if a clock had stopped ticking in my brain. Time dissolved. I had been driven beyond reason, even beyond anger. Inside me, a little boy who had been brutalized was screaming for revenge. A lifetime of provocation, of guilt, had come down to a single instant. There were only two people in the world, and I was one of them. If there were sounds, I didn't hear them.

"You have beaten me for the last time," I told my father, my voice deep and even, "and if you stand in my way, I'll walk right through you. I'm no boy anymore. You have no power over me. You can't stop me. If you hit me now, I'm going to drop you where you stand. For the rest of my life, I'll regret it. But, father or not, I'll punch you out. Now what are *you* going to do?"

I waited, unblinking.

My father, to my astonishment, looked away and lowered his head. I didn't understand. Was he going to try to sucker-punch me? My ears throbbed.

He raised his head, faced me again and said very softly, "Please stay."

"What?" I blurted, confused.

"Please stay, Walter," he said, his shoulders falling. My father seemed to shrink before my eyes. He tried to speak, but no words came. He squeezed my forearm, turned and silently walked into the kitchen.

I looked toward my mother.

"Go talk to him," she whispered, nodding.

I did.

CHAPTER 13

SERGEANT ANDERSON?" called the freshly pressed and polished Duty NCO, a lance corporal who couldn't have been more than nineteen. I glanced at the clock next to my rack in my quarters at the San Diego Marine Corps Recruit Depot. It was 0535 on a Saturday morning in February 1966. *One of the men in my outfit must be in trouble,* I thought. I was the platoon sergeant of a unit of Marines, all of whom were Vietnam veterans and, like me, all short-timers.

"What is it, lance corporal?" I asked.

"The chaplain needs to see you, sarge," he said.

"Anything else?"

"That's all. Just find you."

Such a summons was not welcome news. Somebody was in trouble or sick or had a problem at home. I dressed quickly, not showering. The lance corporal stayed in the doorway.

"You can take off," I told him. "I know where the chaplain is."

"That's OK, sarge," he replied. "I'll walk you over."

Then I knew it was I, not one of my troops, who had the problem. The lance corporal fidgeted, averting his eyes. I suspected by his uneasiness that he had been ordered not to volunteer any information.

"My father?" I asked.

"I don't have any details," he answered. "The chaplain will talk to you about it."

"Is it my father?"

"Yes."

"How bad?" I asked.

"I really don't know."

When we arrived at the chaplain's office, the lance corporal wished me luck. I thanked him and stepped inside. My father was very sick, the chaplain explained. Transportation was being provided to the San Diego airport for a flight to the Los Angeles airport, where I would board a commercial plane to New York.

Two hours later, while awaiting my flight in Los Angeles, I called home. "Daddy didn't make it," my sister-in-law told me. "Bill took him to the Veterans Hospital. He passed away there."

After I hung up the phone, I walked stiffly into a nearby men's room, entered a stall where I could not be seen and cried. I touched my tears, well aware that if I had not walked into the kitchen and talked with him on that leave just six weeks earlier, I may have felt nothing now.

Had he seen death coming? I wondered.

My father had spoken softly that morning, and he had rambled, at one point asking me, "Do you know about *my* mother and father?"

He had never mentioned his parents to me before, but I nodded.

When I was much younger, Carol and Billy had confided to me that both of our father's parents were alcoholics who had died in institutions, his father a suicide. I also knew that, decades earlier, my father had broken the pledge that he and his sister, Dhyne, had made to each other when they were teenagers—that, unlike their parents, they would never drink.

My father spoke unevenly and nervously about his childhood, as if he could not get out what he really wanted to say. Nevertheless, an unmistakable image began to emerge from the fog of his conflicting thoughts: It was of a boy, severely beaten, neglected and abused.

I nodded repeatedly as he spoke, but I asked no questions.

His language was lucid when he changed the subject to his experience in the Army in World War II. He was captured by German troops during the Battle of the Bulge and tortured. He escaped but soon was captured again, taken to a POW camp, tortured again and left to die. He had no recollection of his liberation by American forces. His only memory was of a hospital in England. He weighed just eighty-nine pounds. He had put on some weight by the time he was able to return to the United States, but my mother walked right past him at the train station. She didn't recognize the thin, frail soldier. He then was assigned to West Point, where he taught cadets how to lay line and establish telephone communications. He was honorably discharged and returned to work as an emergency lineman with Con Edison.

In 1954, when I was ten, he was electrocuted during Hurricane Hazel and thrown thirty feet to the ground. The doctors said he'd never climb again. They were wrong. After months in a wheelchair, he returned to Con Edison, climbing poles. He also had saved lives as a volunteer fire captain in Engine 2. He was known all over Westchester County, he boasted. "When I go," he told me, "they'll all be there!"

Because I knew he could not hurt me again, I was able to get beyond the anger that usually clouded my mind when we were together. And as I listened to him open up to me for the first time in his life, I also was able to admit to myself for the first time what, deep inside, I had always suspected: *This man is not my father.*

I was filled with questions I could not ask. *Let it go*, I told myself. *My life is elsewhere.*

"Walter," he told me the morning I left to report to San Diego, "I'm proud of you. Everything you've done—Vietnam, being a sergeant, writing that story in the paper. Everything."

His eyes filled. So did mine.

"And," he added, in the last words I would hear him speak, "I love you."

CHAPTER 14

MY MOTHER shuddered, and her eyes filled.

Why? Why did I have to ask her now if he was my father? Only a few hours earlier, she had buried her husband. What's wrong with me? Say *something*. Why can't I speak?

"No," I still can hear her say slowly. "William Anderson . . . was *not* your father."

My mind seemed to explode into countless fragments of my life, all whirling about: *Here, a book falls to the floor. Over there, a punch in the chest. Carol is waving to me. My mother is crying. A gun is on the car seat. He's saying, "I love you."* I was consumed by scenes from a hundred places and times, all at once, flickering together on a single screen.

Then I heard a voice, *my* voice: "Who *is* my father?"

My mother sighed, and then she spoke: "Honey, I never planned to say anything about your real father and me. I was going to take that secret to my grave." Her words came even more slowly, as if torn from her. "But . . . you deserve to know."

She was sobbing. I reached over and hugged her. After a few minutes, she stopped trembling. I let her go and sat back on the couch, waiting.

Finally, she spoke.

"I fell in love during the war when your . . ." She hesitated, then raised her hands in frustration. "Oh, what do I call him now?"

"Mom," I said softly, "maybe it will be easier for you if you call the man that you married 'my father' and call the other man 'my real father.' I'll know the difference."

"Yes," she said, "that's good."

A few seconds later, her voice a little stronger, she began again:

"We met when I worked at Farrand Optical in Manhattan. I want you to know first that I loved him very much, truly loved him, and he loved me."

She paused.

"His name," she said, "is Albert Dorfman. He had already been separated from his wife for many years when we met. He is Jewish, Walter. And he has another son, named Herbert, who's a couple of years older than Billy."

He is Jewish, Walter. And he has another son . . .

I couldn't seem to respond. I struggled forward against a driving rain of emotions, unable to find my balance.

At last I formed a single sentence, a request: "Mom, please tell me everything."

She nodded.

MY MOTHER CLOSED the bedroom door behind her. She had spoken, and I had listened, for nearly three hours.

I found myself oddly obsessed with my hands. I pinched the flesh on the back of each. Twice I rose off the couch, walked into the tiny bathroom and closely examined my face. It was as if I were seeing *me* for the first time.

"You have your father's piercing eyes," my mother had told me. "But, thank God, your eye color is the same as mine, or Willie would have known you weren't his. You really do look a lot like Al, Walter. You also have his nose, and your forehead and the shape of your face is very similar to his. His lips are fuller than yours, though, and you're a lot taller than he is. His other son, Herb, is also taller than he is."

"Do you have a picture?" I asked.

"No," she replied, "I carried a snapshot of him in my wallet many years ago, but one day Momma saw it. I told her it was a picture of a man I worked with. Momma was shocked. You were about four years old at the time, and your resemblance to Al was obvious. She told me to tear up the picture right away and throw away the pieces. I did, and I wish now I hadn't done that."

"So Grandma knew about my real father?"

"She never talked or acted like she figured it out, but I'm sure she did. She and Grandpa loved you so much, maybe loved you more than they loved anyone. They always said you were the son they never had. Since I had to work, they raised you pretty much as their own child for the first few years of your life. That was before we had to move to Eleventh Avenue and Third Street. You thought Grandma was your mother when you were a baby. You even called her 'Momma.' But the thing is, Grandma never again mentioned the picture to me, and she never *ever* asked me a question."

Alone on the couch now, I was overwhelmed by a tidal wave of conflicted, perplexing, sometimes preposterous thoughts: *If my father is a Jew, am I a Jew too? This morning I had a brother and a sister, but tonight I have two half-brothers and a half-sister. What the hell does "half" mean? Am I half a Jew? Whose fingers are these anyway? Whose hands? Arms? Legs? My brain? Whose brain do I have?*

I tried to call to mind every Jewish person I knew. It was a very short list. There was a tough kid from the neighborhood named Danny whom I had not seen in years. I remembered Dr. Meyer Rabban, the principal of Windward School, and Shapiro and Scheussler, two fellow Marines. *Do I know anyone else?* I smiled. I had almost forgotten Lynn Aaron, a former classmate at A. B. Davis High School. She had told me that her father would not allow her to date me because I was a *goy*, a non-Jew. I chuckled. Her old man was *half* right.

OK, who else?

Suddenly, it came to me: I knew other Jews, only not in person. I had found their books when I was a small boy, learning on my own in the Mount Vernon Public Library, and later as a young Marine still irresistibly drawn to reading. They lived vividly in my head, writers like Herman Wouk and Norman Mailer and Irving Wallace and Elie Wiesel.

But I don't know them personally.

I was never more alone; I was never less alone. My thoughts cascaded uncontrollably. *My mother had an affair, or I wouldn't be here. I have another father. And another brother too! I'm a Jew—by half. Am I like anybody else? Is anybody else like me? Who am I now?*

I couldn't seem to hold fast. Whatever lucid ideas and logical conclusions I possessed were quickly consumed in the hot lava of raw emotion. A carnival of people, the players of my life, materialized before me—sometimes the same people at different ages.

I'm losing it.

Tears started to well up, yet I began to smile. I pictured my mother saying good night to me, and I could almost hear again her last words, "Walter, you were meant to be."

At last, I relaxed. *I can sleep now. I know what I have to do, and I'll begin tomorrow.*

I closed my eyes.

CHAPTER 15

THE STORY my mother told me begins in December 1943. Although no bombs had landed on United States soil in the two years since Pearl Harbor, Americans vigorously searched their skies and patrolled their shorelines and harbors. The words of war were in their conversations, in their newspapers, in their movie theaters, in the news heard every night on their radio stations. The massive life-and-death struggle waged across Europe and Asia touched every loaf of bread purchased in their corner stores and every pint of gasoline rationed at their local service stations. It called to their sons, their brothers, their husbands and their fathers to serve in uniform. The impersonal fury of it all became crushingly personal for some Americans when they opened telegrams that reported their loved ones missing or killed in action. Truly, it was a time of sacrifice and hope, of villains and heroes.

In this titanic struggle of good and evil, with the fate of much of the human race in peril, vast power was exercised on a global scale. For decades to come, historians would chronicle the World War II years in wide sweeps, describing in voluminous detail the strategies; the victories and the defeats; the stirring words of prime ministers and presidents, generals and admirals.

In the basement apartment at 174 Rich Avenue in Mount Vernon, New York, however, the challenge my mother faced was local and immediate. Mrs. Ethel Anderson needed bread for her family, and she was broke.

"Momma," she called out from the bathroom, "do we have any money set aside?"

"A little, Ethel. What do you need?"

"Can Poppa pick up some bread from the grocery store? He can charge it if he has to. I get paid Friday."

"We'll get what we can," replied her mother. "Be sure to wear the gray wool scarf. The radio says we're going to get some snow. It's cold outside."

Ethel nodded and continued to brush her hair. She studied her face in the mirror and wondered, *Am I pretty?* She was thirty-one years old. The births of her two children—Billy, who was twelve, and Carol, who was six—had not softened her body. At five feet three, she was curvy and compact and full-breasted and, she observed with some pride, still had the firm legs of a dancer. Her brown hair was cut medium length, like every other woman's she knew. Each of her large hazel eyes had a distinct gold ring curiously circling a dark pupil. Her nose was unexceptional, small and straight—but, if she clenched her jaw just right, she could make her cheeks dimple. *Pretty?* She wasn't sure.

What she did know was that she was about to lie to her mother, and her face flushed with guilt.

"Momma," she said, "I have to work late tonight. I'll probably miss dinner. OK?"

"How late?" asked her mother.

"I don't think I'll be too late," she replied. "Maybe a couple of hours."

"If it's only a couple of hours," her mother said, "then I'll save something, so you can eat when you come home."

"OK, Momma."

A few minutes later, Ethel was riding the bus across Mount Vernon to the subway in the Bronx for the rest of the trip to lower Manhattan. Dawn, she knew, was only a distant promise this early in the morning. She wouldn't see the sun rise until the train neared Harlem. The streetlamps looked like lonely little islands on the otherwise dark blocks, the glow of each forming a ring of dull yellow light on the pavement below.

Seated alone on the bus, watching streetlamp after streetlamp pass by, she again felt the confusion that had been building for the last couple of weeks: Why, she asked herself, had she agreed to see Al again tonight? She knew she had to stop thinking about him. She concentrated, forcing herself to picture other people: Tiny images of Billy and Carol and Momma and Poppa began to materialize, only to burst into dust, popping like balloons when Al's face suddenly returned, more vivid than before.

To MANUFACTURE bombsights used by America's pilots during the war, Farrand Optical Company rented workspace for its employees in the Harriet Hubbard Ayer Building at 317 East 34th Street in Manhattan, and my mother was one of the many war wives trained to finely grind the lenses used in those devices.

Her shop steward, Albert Dorfman, was a slender man about five feet seven inches tall. His jet-black hair crowned an oval face of fair complexion with three prominent features: a straight nose, full lips and dark-brown eyes—eyes that glistened behind long black eyelashes. *Penetrating* eyes, my mother told me many times over the years—eyes that pinned her to the moment, made her heart beat faster, touched her, confused her.

Whenever Al focused on Ethel, when their eyes met, she was riveted. Always, she saw his eyes. In her dreams, she saw his eyes.

Even more, he listened to her. He *heard* her.

ETHEL WANTED to please Al, but she was so afraid. What if somebody saw her sitting in the lobby of the hotel? She wondered whether Al understood just how frightened she was.

She raised her head and looked across the room to the front desk, where Al was speaking to the clerk, an elderly man whose movements, even from where she sat, seemed glacial. She kneaded the gray wool scarf on her lap. What was she doing in this place? My mother recalled how, embarrassed, her face had begun to redden and she told herself, "This is crazy. I'm married!"

"Married?" she asked herself quietly, and then my mother began to silently reflect on her own question. She knew her husband had a girl-friend and, she recalled bitterly, he had brought this woman into his home, *her* home. She had challenged the girlfriend at the time: "If you want him, you can have him."

A chill ran up her spine, and she shuddered. She wasn't seated in this hotel to punish her husband, she knew. She was here because of her feelings for Al—compelled, drawn to the moment. Still, her fear grew second by second.

She turned her head so she could see the brass and glass revolving door that led to the street. If only she could bolt from the lobby as fast as her legs could carry her, maybe the fear would go away. She began to rise. Then Al turned from the counter—almost as if he could hear her thoughts—smiled and made a small sign with his hand to signal that he'd be finished in a minute or so.

AL CLOSED THE DOOR to the hotel room behind them, reached back and secured the safety latch. He touched her shoulder. She was trembling.

"Don't be afraid," he said.

CHAPTER 16

M Y MOTHER skipped the details of her night with my real father, of course, while reliving them in her mind. Then, catching her breath, she continued her story. Incredibly, I thought, my mother could still recall conversations she'd had with Al more than twenty years before, as if they'd spoken only yesterday. She began by describing a particularly troubling discussion.

"I've missed my period only twice before," she told Al, "and that was for Billy and Carol. It's only a couple of weeks, but I'm like clockwork—*never* late unless I'm pregnant. So, yes, I'm sure I'm pregnant."

It was lunchtime in Manhattan, and they sat facing each other across a small table in the rear of a Third Avenue delicatessen. The place was filling quickly.

"I believe you," he said, "and I'm going to help you."

"Help *us*," she corrected.

"Of course," he agreed. *"Us."*

"I want you to know . . . ," she began, but stopped abruptly when the waitress arrived with their sandwich plates. Both sat silently until the waitress finished her delivery and returned to the counter.

"Al," she said, "I want you to know that I love you, that I never knew what love could be until you . . ."

"Ethel," he interrupted, "I . . ."

"No," she stopped him, "don't say it now unless . . ."

"Unless I mean it?"

"Yes, Al, unless you really mean it."

"I love you, Ethel. I do love you."

IT BEGAN TO FEEL, my mother told me, as if she were standing on two logs that were slowly drifting apart. Sometimes she'd find herself day-dreaming, reflecting on her intimate moments with Al: "So this is love," she'd say to herself. "It *is* beautiful." Al seemed to care so much about her, and she ached for him. Then she'd see Willie in uniform, the country at war, and Billy and Carol, who looked so much like him and . . .

She wished she could have talked to her mother or her sisters, she said, but she knew she couldn't. She carried too much guilt, and she was ashamed.

My mother was hesitant to tell me what happened next, she said. "Please go on," I encouraged her. She described how Al had assured her that he had a solution that would be "best for everyone": She was married with a son and a daughter; he was still married and had a son. Yes, too many people to hurt.

As Al waited in the doctor's reception area, my mother explained, she carefully followed the instructions he had given her. The words were *very* important, he had insisted, especially what *not* to say: "Do *not* say you're pregnant. *Absolutely* do not say you want an abortion. It's all fixed with the doctor. You tell him you have 'female troubles'. He'll examine you, and then he'll advise you that he thinks he needs to perform a dilatation and curettage—a 'D and C'—and he'll suggest that you schedule an appointment with his receptionist for later this week."

When the physician asked his last question, as expected, he told Ethel that the receptionist would be able to make a time for her.

"Thank you," she said.

Finally, she told me, she knew what she was going to do.

She brushed past the receptionist, took Al by the hand as he was rising from his chair and led him past the doctor's outer door and into the hallway.

"What are you doing?" he asked, clearly astonished.

"I'm going to have the baby," she said.

When the elevator reached the lobby, she led Al to a leather couch near the doorman's desk. They sat side by side.

"Why?" he asked, raising his hands, palms up. "I don't understand. What happened in there?"

"Nothing happened in there, Al," she said, then pointed to her chest: "It happened *here*."

"I don't understand."

She then smiled at Al, she said, and my mother smiled at me as she continued.

"I want this baby," she told Al. "I didn't know how much until I faced the doctor. Look," she said, grasping both of his hands, "I know you're worried. I am too, but I know what I'm doing. I love you, but I know I can't have you—not the right way. I'm married and, whatever else my husband is, he's still the father of my two children. He wouldn't let me go anyway, no matter what. And if he suspected I was pregnant with another man's baby . . . well, I'm afraid he'd kill the baby *and* me."

Al started to raise his hands.

"No," she said, stopping him before he could speak. "Don't say anything, Al. Not *now*. Just listen until I finish. I know that I can't have you—but I can have part of you all the rest of my life. Every time I see your child, I'll see you. But there's one thing I need you to do."

"What is that?" he asked.

"You have to promise that this child stays our secret."

He hesitated.

"Please, Al. *Promise*."

He squeezed her hands lightly, then smiled.

"I will," he said.

CHAPTER 17

THE BABY'S not breathing," my mother heard the nurse say. "He's blue."

"What's happening to my baby?" she demanded, trying to lift herself from the table in the delivery room of Mount Vernon Hospital.

"Honey, he's going to be all right," the nurse said. "We're putting him into cold water and warm water, and he'll . . ."

Then I screamed, my mother told me. Though relieved that I was OK, she said, she still was worried. Nearly nine months before, after she discovered she was pregnant, my mother had been sure to have sex with her husband when he came home on leave from the Army camp in New Jersey. Later, after Willie had been shipped off to Europe, she had written to him with the news that he'd be a father again. Now, after all that planning, she prayed that her baby boy's appearance wouldn't betray her.

"Please," she pleaded to the nurse, "let me see him." And she prayed.

God, please don't let him look too much like Al. Please, no brown eyes. If he has my eye color, I can always say he looks like a Crolly. The Crolly side has dark hair—but not Al's brown eyes, please God.

The nurse gently placed the baby in Ethel's arms.

She looked at him lovingly and smiled, tears rolling down her cheeks.

Thank you, God.

A WEEK LATER, on September 7, 1944, the *Daily Argus* announced several births in its "Mr. Stork Presents Today" column, including: "Walter Herman Anderson, born to Private and Mrs. William H. Anderson, 174 Rich Avenue, Aug. 31. Mrs. Anderson is the former Ethel Crolly."

My mother told me she thought it ironic that her two sons would forever share the same birthday: Billy had come into the world exactly thirteen years earlier.

THE MAN who thought he was my father had been promoted to corporal about the same time that I entered the world. But those two events were his last pleasant experiences during the war, William Anderson had told me on the last day I saw him alive. Sitting in this same apartment, he had described in detail what he remembered of the two years that followed my birth.

Almost four months after I was born, he told me—while assigned to a field artillery unit of the 106th Infantry Division in the Ardennes in France—he was summoned early one morning to see his commanding officer, a captain.

Communications had suddenly failed, said the captain. No one knew why. At thirty-five, Corporal "Whitey" Anderson was both the oldest man in the unit and—because of his civilian experience as an emergency lineman in New York—the most knowledgeable soldier in the outfit. The captain ordered him to take one of the trucks, ride the lines, find the break and fix it.

"I'll ride with you, Whitey," the captain said.

The two men found a damaged line in a valley about half a mile from camp, and the corporal reported, "The line's been cut, sir, but I can fix it." He strapped a wheel of line to his shoulder, checked his tool belt, tightened his spikes and quickly climbed the pole. At the top, he froze.

"Christ!" he shouted down. "Germans everywhere!"

He was on the ground in three steps, and he and the captain dove together into a culvert to hide. It was futile. The two were surrounded in minutes by hundreds of enemy soldiers. They were captured, stripped of their winter coats, and their hands were bound tightly behind their backs with wire. The air was frigid, and they trembled in the cold.

They were beaten bloody, marched to a small camp, beaten again and forced into a temporary cage made from barbed wire.

An hour later, the captain was dragged about twenty yards along the ground by his shirt collar, pulled to his feet and then interrogated. The corporal couldn't make out the questions—but at one point he saw the captain stiffen and shake his head *no*. The German soldier who was questioning him then raised a pistol and shot the captain in the face. His body collapsed to the ground.

I'm next, Corporal Anderson told himself.

But no one came for him. He saw that there was a lot of activity in the little camp, with German soldiers passing through quickly. The wire cut into his wrists, but there was space between his hands. He began twisting his fists, ignoring the pain, working the wire. *It has to give*, he thought. He felt a wire snap, and the restraint loosened.

Still no one came. He was given no food, no water. He sat quietly. As the afternoon passed, the size of the enemy unit shrank dramatically. By dark, only a few German troops remained in the makeshift camp. The lone soldier assigned to guard him leaned against the corner post of his cage. The corporal—certain that, sooner or later, he'd be killed—unwound the wire, then moved silently behind the enemy soldier. He slipped the wire around the guard's neck and garroted him so quickly and with such force that the only sound was the single slap of the man's hands to his neck.

The corporal opened the wire door and dragged the guard's body into the cage. He removed the soldier's heavy overcoat and helmet, dressed himself, picked up the man's rifle, then walked out of the camp and into the night.

ADOLF HITLER CALLED his December 1944 offensive in the Ardennes "Autumn Mist"; the Allies called it "the Battle of the Bulge." Ultimately, more than a million Allied and German soldiers were engaged in this, Hitler's last-ditch assault. By the time it drew to a close in January 1945, with the Allied forces victorious, nineteen thousand American soldiers had been killed, forty-seven thousand had been wounded, and fifteen thousand had been captured. The 106th Infantry Division, Corporal Anderson's outfit, suffered devastating losses.

Anderson, though, knew only that he was a soldier alone, deep behind enemy lines. He was sure that he'd be hunted for killing a German soldier. The first night and day, he told me, were the most difficult. He hid in a rocky hedgerow, chilled to the bone. His muscles, bruised and swollen from the beating, stiffened. He didn't stretch a limb. Nor did he stand to relieve himself. He feared that the slightest move might disclose his position. So he lay still as the stones, and the pain was indescribable.

In the dark of the second night, he rose and made his way across a field, the cold ground crunching under his feet. The noise alarmed him, but a growing hunger and the need to sleep drove him forward. He came upon a farm, slipped into its barn and climbed up into the hayloft. He squeezed into a corner mound and then fell into a deep sleep. He awoke several hours later, aching with hunger. He peeked through a knothole in the barn. It was light outside, so it had to be daytime. The German soldiers had stolen his watch. *Was it morning or afternoon?* No matter, he had to find food—and if he had to kill for it, he would.

Fortunately, there was no one in the farmer's home. He ate hurriedly in the kitchen and then quickly explored the house. He found a heavy shirt and a civilian overcoat in a hall closet, changed clothes and then stuffed the pockets of the farmer's overcoat with potatoes and bread. He had been in the house only minutes. Outside, he could make out the boom of artillery fire in the distance.

His body hunched over, he walked along a hedgerow and buried the German soldier's overcoat under some brush. Finally, he made his way into a patch of woods.

Over the next three days and nights, walking carefully at night, he eluded the German troops—but he was becoming weaker.

He was asleep in another barn on the morning of the sixth day when he felt himself being prodded. He heard voices shouting in what sounded like German. He sat up with a start. He was surrounded by armed civilians, each with a rifle pointed at him. He raised his hands. One of the men, yelling louder than the others, kept pointing to his head. Then he understood: *It's my blond hair and blue eyes. They think I'm a German-American who has turned on his own people.* And that was his last thought before a rifle butt knocked him unconscious.

When he came to, his hands and feet were bound, and he was bouncing on the floor bed in the back of a truck.

He was imprisoned first in Stalag 8 in Ziegenheim and then moved a few weeks later to Stalag 9 at Bad Orb. Some time after arriving at the second camp, he was chosen by the German guards to be a disciplinary example for the other prisoners. He was beaten with truncheons and then separated from his fellow American soldiers. He received neither food nor water. His fellow prisoners, unable to help him, were forced to watch him slowly starve.

His last memory of the prisoner-of-war camp, he told me, was of a fly on his face. He was too weak to raise his hand to swat it away.

On March 30, 1945, he later learned, Allied forces liberated Stalag 9. Several other American soldiers carefully lifted their comatose colleague, Corporal William Anderson, onto a stretcher. Emaciated—his muscles withered and his bones nearly visible beneath his wasted skin— he weighed less than ninety pounds.

He did not regain consciousness until several days later in a London hospital. When his eyes opened, he told me, he saw white-on-white: *White sheets. White walls. White ceilings. White ladies in white.*

"Are you an angel?" he asked a nurse.

AFTER ALMOST four weeks of hospitalization, Corporal William Anderson was told he was ready to return home to the United States. He arrived in New York by ship on May 5, 1945. The Army immediately promoted him to sergeant and ordered him to West Point, where he served as an instructor in communications and field artillery. By the time he was honorably discharged on October 30, 1945, he had earned four battle stars: Rhineland, Ardennes, Central Europe and the Siegfried Line.

MY MOTHER told me it was obvious that her husband had changed in ways she did not understand. Because of his diminished physical appearance, she had not recognized him at first in the crowd of returning veterans arriving at Penn Station in Manhattan. In time, he grew back into his muscular body again. Willie looked like himself, she said, but he was not the same.

My mother said she knew that her husband had abruptly ended his relationship with his girlfriend—the woman she derisively called "Old Piano Legs" and with whom, my mother was certain, he'd had a child before entering the service. And there were the sores on Willie's legs that would not heal—an enduring consequence, the doctors said, of his prisoner-of-war experience. Yet, oddly, he showed neither discomfort from the breakup nor pain from the sores. "It was as if," she told me, "he did not feel."

The most frightening change, though, was his drinking. Prior to the war, he'd have a beer from time to time; now Willie would buy whiskey. And, as he drank, he would grow meaner by the moment. An old friend of her husband, a fellow emergency lineman, confided his concern that "Willie wasn't the same since he came back," that he was hurting other men in bar fights.

One night, my mother reminded Willie of his parents' troubles with liquor and of the pledge of abstinence that he and his sister had taken. "Shut up!" he bellowed, then punched her shoulder so hard that she fell to the floor.

He had struck her several times before the war, but not with such force or malevolent intent.

And there was the morning when Billy, then fourteen, was playfully wrestling with his father on the living-room rug. Suddenly, inexplicably, Willie's face turned red, his eyes narrowed, and he angrily overpowered Billy and began to methodically pound the boy's head into a radiator. Ethel screamed and leaped onto her enraged husband. He tossed her off easily, but it was enough—fortunately—to stop the assault on Billy.

～

FEAR OF HER husband's violence, my mother explained, made visits with my real father perilous and, consequently, rare. She told me about her first meeting with Al after my birth, their conversations still fresh in her mind.

It was an October afternoon in 1946. They were standing near the clock in Grand Central Terminal as shoppers and commuters swirled hurriedly about them. Anyone watching would have seen the man open his arms, inviting the small boy. My mother said I glanced at her and then, without hesitation, reached for my real father, though he was a stranger to me.

"I think he looks like me," Al observed, lightly squeezing me to his chest, "but he has *your* eye color."

My mother laughed, then said with a smile, "I thought I told you that!"

"How much time do we have?" Al asked.

"A few hours," she replied.

"We can walk a little," he suggested, "then maybe take a table in the automat."

My mother said she then studied the man holding her child, *their* child. Al had not seen his son before because it hadn't seemed safe enough before—and, she admitted to herself, she was confounded by her own feelings. Much had happened since the baby was born. She believed she still loved Al, but her concern for her young son's safety was genuine. Tormented by worry that her husband might stumble upon the truth, gripped by guilt and goaded by fear, she vowed to some-how make the marriage work. She was determined to learn to live with Willie, whoever he had become. Although she and Al had spoken sever-al times during the last two years over the telephone, she had resisted this day.

But now, studying the two as the father played silly hand games with his son, my mother said, she was certain she had made the right decision.

Once they were seated in the automat, they had a conversation unlike any before. The dam collapsed. My mother described her life now that she no longer worked at Farrand Optical—her hopes, her marriage and how she was determined to make it all work out. Al told her about his divorce after years of separation, spoke candidly about the younger woman he had pledged to marry and spelled out his business plans. He squeezed Ethel's hand. Her eyes filled. Though his voice was unsteady, Al spoke with pride about his son Herbert, who was eighteen, *and* his son Walter, who was seated comfortably on his lap. Raising a water glass, he toasted long life and success for both boys. And in that moment, my mother said, she and Al found unexpected joy, as if they had discovered each other anew.

"I love you," he told her.

AFTER PAUSING, a smile on her face at the memory of that moment, my mother recalled for me the scene later that afternoon as the three of us waited together in Grand Central for the train that would take her and her son back to Mount Vernon. Her story began with me happily playing in my father's arms.

"He's a Jewish boy," Al said softly, almost to himself.

"Do you mean," Ethel asked, smiling, "like father, like son?"

He raised his eyebrows, agreeing.

"I had him baptized a Protestant," Ethel continued, "but I also made sure he was circumcised."

Al chuckled. "So you think *that* makes him Jewish!"

"No," she said. "*You* make him Jewish. But I had to do something—and that was something I could do. He's the first Anderson to be circumcised."

"He'll be forever grateful, Ethel."

Both of them burst into laughter, and the little boy—feeling their joy—happily joined in.

"See," Al said, pointing to the child. "I told you so!"

The crowd around them was thickening. More people were scurrying through their gate.

Al and Ethel became silent, struggling to hold the moment and knowing that time was getting short.

When Al looked again into the boy's eyes, he saw his own eyes— only in a different color—looking back. "This is one Jewish boy," he said, breaking the silence, "who is not going to be hurt because he is a Jew."

My mother said her eyes welled with tears. She touched Al's cheek lightly, and her little boy, imitating her, did the same.

Then, she said, she reached for me. It was time.

CHAPTER 18

MY EYES OPENED at 0530. The only sound I could hear in my mother's living room was the steady ticking of a small illuminated clock. I paused momentarily in the darkness, gathering myself. Her bedroom door was closed, so it was safe to flick on the lamp. *I have a lot to do today*, I thought to myself. *But my head's still spinning from last night. I can still almost hear her voice telling me about the real father I never knew. Can't think straight. Maybe I should work out a little to clear my head.*

I rose off the couch and began to forage in my canvas bag for a pair of sweatpants. I heard Andy, my mother's dog, make a whiny sound from behind her bedroom door, then apparently lose interest and go quiet again. I slipped on a pair of sneakers, wedged the apartment key in my sock and quietly slipped out.

When I pushed open the front door to the apartment building, the frigid air hit me like a slap. I shivered uncontrollably. After a tour in Vietnam followed by orders to the Marine base in sunny San Diego, I wasn't ready for the bite of a New York winter. Quickly, I started doing jumping jacks and push-ups to get warm before I started to run. The street was empty. *Oh, expecting company at five-thirty in the morning?* I thought, and laughed.

After about half a mile, the shivering ceased and I settled into an easy pace. As the webs slowly began to dissolve, the first coherent thought to emerge was a recollection of the difficult promise my mother had asked me to make the night before.

"Please keep my secret," she had pleaded with me. "For as long as Billy and Carol are alive, please, *please* don't ever tell either of them, especially Billy, about your father. It would shock Carol, but it would devastate Billy. He'd never forgive me, and he'd never look at you the same way. He can't help himself. He's his father's son. But he's my son too, my firstborn. *Promise me?*"

When I hesitated, she asked again for my promise. "Please?" she said, her voice shaky.

I stayed silent, a dull ache in my chest. She may have been right about Billy, but I knew I desperately wanted to tell Carol. We had always trusted each other. I kept her secrets, and she kept mine. I was uncomfortable that I had to hide this news—the biggest secret of all— from my sister, but I had never seen my mother so frightened. *What do I do?*

"OK," I agreed at last, reluctantly. "I won't tell Carol or Billy."

"Not ever?"

"Not *ever*, Mom."

She relaxed, visibly relieved, then asked, "Are you going to try to look up your real father?"

"I don't know, Mom. Do you *want* me to find him?"

"No," she said. "Just the opposite. I'd be relieved if you *don't* go looking for him. I have no idea what you'd find after all these years, and I'd rather that you didn't search at all. If you did find him or your other brother, Herb, this could all blow up, and Carol and Billy might find out."

My feet thudded gently on the pavement. It was getting brighter outside. The streetlamps were turning themselves off. I began to focus again, as I had so many times the night before, on this mysterious man—my father, Albert Dorfman.

I'm sure he remembers me. Mom said he saw me a few more times after that first meeting in Grand Central when I was two years old. But I have no memory of him. And the last time Mom spoke to him was over the telephone when I was ten.

"It wasn't that Al didn't want to see you," she had insisted passionately during our conversation, the tears rolling down her cheeks. "I stopped him. I pleaded with him when you were ten years old not to call anymore, and I refused to let him see you again. It had gotten too dangerous. Willie had gotten worse. You know how bad he got, Walter. I tried to shield you as best as I could. Willie would have killed you if he even suspected that you were somebody else's child."

Did he suspect I wasn't his? Is that why he beat me? Well, if he had any doubts, they must have been unconscious, because Mom said he never raised the question to her.

"Don't blame Al for not seeing you more," my mother added. "It was *my* decision, not Al's. I closed him off. I turned him away to protect you."

"Mom, I really do understand," I said, squeezing her hand.

"Are you sure?" she asked.

I smiled and nodded. "Mom, I'm OK," I told her. "More than OK, believe me. Maybe someday I'll be able to look for these people."

"Thank you," she said, adding nervously, "I know I've asked you to do something very difficult."

"Yes, you have," I agreed. "But I'll keep my word."

"I know you will, honey," she said, relieved.

I WAS RUNNING easily now, my footfalls in a steady rhythm. Suddenly, to my surprise, I realized that I had inadvertently jogged across Mount Vernon to Scott's Bridge, which spanned the New Haven Railroad tracks. I was only two blocks from Eleventh Avenue and Third Street.

Oh, hell, you're almost there. Keep going.

Suddenly I was incredibly alert, aware of every crack in the pavement, the siding peeling off some of the houses, the trash scattered about a decrepit gas station, the boards covering the windows of a long-closed candy store. I passed the playground at Grimes School and, a half-block later, the house where Barry Williams used to live. Then I was *there*, at the stoop of 159 South Eleventh Avenue, the tenement where I had spent my childhood. For a few seconds, I felt nothing. Then I exploded.

I'm free!

I threw my arms in the air, like a sports fan cheering. A passing motorist waved, mistakenly assuming I was sending him a friendly early-morning greeting. I laughed.

I'm really free!

My mind was flooding with vivid images, as it had been the night before, but this time I was neither overwhelmed nor confused. I was clear and warm, despite the chill, and I was filled with joy. I let the scenes play out, and slowly an idea—the beginning of an important understanding—started to surface. I could almost grasp the thought.

I am . . . well, whoever I am, I'm better off today than I was yesterday. At least now I know who I'm not.

Suddenly, a memory flickered. I could almost see myself as a teenager, dropping my manuscript into a garbage pail behind this tenement.

I know who I want to be.

I silently made a vow to myself: *I'm going to write again.*

I took one last, long look at the stoop and started my jog back to Locust Street.

Whoever I am, whoever I'll be, everything changes today.

THREE HOURS LATER, I sent a telegram to General Wallace M. Greene Jr., the Commandant of the Marine Corps. I asked him to transfer me, for personal reasons, to a post in New York. Within forty-eight hours, I received a call from the commanding officer of the Navy and Marine Armory in New Rochelle. He told me I had been assigned to his command, a reserve unit, and he wanted me to report to his office on Monday morning.

"Yes, sir," I said.

"Do you know where we are, sergeant?" the captain asked.

"Yes, sir, I do," I replied. New Rochelle adjoined Mount Vernon, and the armory was no more than twenty minutes by car from my mother's apartment.

When I arrived at his office at 0700 on Monday morning, the captain asked if I had thought about becoming a reservist now that my enlistment was coming to a close. "Sir," I said, "when the papers arrive in a few weeks, I'm going to be a civilian again. After more than four and a half years on active duty, sir, I don't think I want to be an active reservist. . . . But if I change my mind, sir, I'll let you know."

He laughed and then assigned me to lead the reserve troops in physical training the following weekend. He told me to check in with the first sergeant twice a week after that, until my papers arrived.

"Sir," I asked, "does this mean that I'm free to look for a job?"

"Yes," he said, "but don't forget that you are an active-duty United States Marine until you get your papers. Do *nothing* to embarrass yourself or the Marine Corps."

"Yes, sir," I said.

One morning, a few weeks later, the first sergeant informed me that my papers had arrived. I immediately drove to the armory, signed the necessary documents and shook the first sergeant's hand, then the captain's.

"*Mister* Anderson," the captain called out as I turned to leave.

"Yes, sir?"

"You're going to do all right," he said.

CHAPTER 19

CITIZENS WERE TEARING at each other. The country's involvement in Vietnam was angrily and increasingly debated in every corner of the United States. The arguments blanketed the nation like a noxious gas. The din was becoming inescapable; civil disturbances were growing more heated. Slowly, I had become frustrated, and then hurt, by the hostile remarks toward veterans by some of my fellow Americans. What had started as an irritation in December of 1965, when I returned from Southeast Asia, had become increasingly painful for me by March of 1966. The words stung terribly.

Like the Marines I served with, I had expected my country to provide the privacy and freedom I needed to make a life for myself. Instead, when my military experience had to be disclosed—in job interviews, in particular—too often some of my countrymen simply could not resist volunteering to me, unsolicited, their opinions about the war.

The most obnoxious of the critics sometimes went a step further. They would describe, with neither encouragement nor information from me, what they *believed* had been my experience in Vietnam. And then, invariably, they would generously offer their "sympathy." I wanted none of it.

One personnel interviewer at a large company in Manhattan even asked me why I had decided to go to Vietnam, as if I had chosen an odd way to spend a summer vacation. And then—not waiting for a reply— he proceeded to advise me, fervently and at length, why I had made a mistake serving there. When he had finished, he folded his arms across his chest and sat quietly, his eyes focused on my face, awaiting my response.

I decided not to reply directly.

"In the neighborhood where I grew up," I told him, "most of the families were black."

"What has that got to do with . . . ?" he interrupted, and his tone was impatient.

I raised my hand, silencing him.

"And," I continued, "I remember an expression that seems to fit right now: 'When white folks and black folks get together, they talk about black folks.' You're sitting with a Vietnam veteran, so—what?— let's talk about Vietnam? I suppose you're going to tell me next that some of your best friends are Vietnam veterans."

He shifted nervously in his chair, averting my eyes.

"Look at me," I said firmly in the tone of voice I would have used to call a platoon to attention.

Instantly, our eyes locked.

"Sooner or later," I said, "this war will end. And here's what you'll be left with: nothing but your arrogance. You think you know all about me? You couldn't begin to understand why I joined the Marines, and I don't have to explain to you why I served in Vietnam. That's none of your business. All you need to understand is that I served honorably. I came here for a job but, to tell you the truth, right now I'd rather kick your ass."

"No!" he blurted, pushing himself and his chair away from his desk. He was trapped.

I chuckled and then shook my head.

"You're not going to get hurt today," I told him softly. "You see, I'm not what you think I am. I just wanted to see your face without the smirk."

"I'm sorry," he said.

"Yes," I replied. "I'm sure you are. You'll also be very happy when I leave your office."

And I'm sure he was.

I EAGERLY LOOKED FORWARD to my first job, as a technician at Nevis Laboratories, a division of Columbia University. The pay was low, less than ninety dollars a week, but I'd have the chance to attend college classes tuition-free after a probationary period. At long last, after dozens of interviews, my military experience had become a plus: The personnel officer told me I had qualified for the opportunity because of the electronics schools I had attended in the Marines. Nevis was located along the Hudson River in Irvington, New York. I still lived with my mother in Mount Vernon, less than a half hour from the labs, so it was an easy commute.

This is my shot, I thought. *I'll do the work, whatever they want done, and I'll go to college in the off-hours.*

On the first day, a supervisor explained my duties as a technician: I would serve as an assistant to the researchers, professors and scientists who measured the results of atomic-particle experiments conducted at Nevis. I could expect to solder connections, read gauges, record readings and the like—in other words, the stuff of tedium.

I noticed almost immediately that some of the lab personnel relished arguing their views loudly about the ongoing fighting in Vietnam—a mere thread of the larger debate spreading across the country—and I was dismayed to hear military service disdained by some of them. I decided to keep to myself, as I had learned to do years before in Windward School, to avoid confrontation.

Their minds are made up. Don't let them under your skin. Remember, discipline.

I had started on a Monday. On Thursday morning, one of the talkers spoke directly to me: "I heard you were a Marine in Vietnam. Is that true?"

"Yes," I replied.

"What did you do there?"

"I was a sergeant."

His eyes widened, the surprise naked on his face. After more than four and a half years in the Marine Corps, I still was only twenty-one—and I looked even younger.

"A *sergeant?*"

"Yes."

"Well, come on now, tell us about it."

"No, I don't think so."

He persisted for several minutes, even after one of the scientists told him to stop. And I continued to listen politely. *Discipline,* I had to remind myself.

Finally, he took a breath.

"No," I said again, firmly, then turned away to resume my work. I was seething. *I hope he spins me around. If he does, he's going down.*

He stood awkwardly for several seconds, nonplused by the curtness of my response. Then he walked away, mumbling to himself.

Over the next few days, the decibel level of the Vietnam debate seemed to lower somewhat on the floor. Another problem began to surface, though: One of the researchers repeatedly referred to me as "the boy."

Finally, he addressed me directly: "*Boy,* can you . . . ?"

"Excuse me," I interrupted. Speaking softly enough so that others could not hear me, I pointed to the name on my ID badge. "That's me, sir: Walter Anderson. I would appreciate it if you would call me 'Walter,' but 'Anderson' is OK if you like. But please don't call me 'boy.' I'm sure you don't mean it to be insulting, but it's insulting to me. Now, sir, how can I help you?"

He asked me to separate and solder some color-coded components.

"Yes, sir," I said.

He began to turn away, changed his mind, then leaned over me and spoke loud enough for the other workers to hear: "And I want this done now, *boy*! Do you understand?"

I was genuinely surprised. After all, I had been courteous and clear. When I turned on my stool to face him, he pressed his finger into my chest and repeated himself: "Understand, *boy*?"

I reached up and squeezed his right hand, then quickly twisted the hand back into his wrist.

"Ow!" he grunted.

"That hurts, doesn't it?" I asked softly.

"Please," he pleaded. He held himself up by bracing his left hand on the workbench, but the pain disabled him. He was helpless.

"Does it hurt?" I asked again.

"Yes," he answered quickly. "Please let me go."

"Words hurt too," I said, then released him.

I walked into the personnel office a few minutes later and requested that I be paid out to that day.

"Why?" the personnel officer asked me.

"I'm pretty sure I just quit," I replied.

I'M RIGHT BACK WHERE I STARTED, I thought to myself as I drove back to my mother's apartment in Mount Vernon. *Dammit! Now I have to go through more of those awful interviews. Why did that bastard have to call me "boy"?*

It was late in the morning, and traffic was light on the Saw Mill River Parkway. I continued to fume, and I was speeding.

I should have dropped him.

The music on the car radio was interrupted by news of another anti-Vietnam protest. I turned off the radio and drove onto the side of the road. I turned off the ignition, put my head in my hands and sat quietly.

I'm too angry to drive. I'll kill somebody.

Minutes passed, then I heard tapping on the glass. It was a police officer. I hadn't noticed his car pull up behind mine or seen his flashing lights.

What now?

When I rolled down the window, he asked if I needed assistance.

"No," I said. "I just decided to stop for a little while."

"Can I see your license and registration?"

He examined the documents and then returned both.

"Thank you," he said.

I nodded.

"Why did you pull to the side?"

"I was too mad to drive," I replied. "I'm OK now."

"Why were you so mad?"

Should I tell him? Oh, what the hell. The story flooded forth, from start to finish. I needed badly to tell someone—and, well, he'd asked.

The officer shook my hand, and he *meant* the handshake.

"Good for you," he said, smiling broadly.

MY MOTHER was at her job as a telephone switchboard supervisor at Gimbel's in the Yonkers Cross County Shopping Center, so her apartment was empty when I arrived home in the middle of the workday. I sat alone on her couch. My mind was swirling.

I don't get it. People screw with you and then expect that nothing will happen to them.

My adjustment to civilian life was not going smoothly. In the final two and a half years of my enlistment, I had been in precisely one fist-fight with another Marine. But I already had been in three clashes with civilians in the past few weeks—and that wasn't counting the researcher who had called me "boy."

One of those clashes had been particularly senseless. About a month earlier, I had joined my brother Bill for a beer at a bar on the south side of Mount Vernon. At the other end of the bar that night sat a truck driver well on his way to being drunk. For no apparent reason, he decided to leave his small group of cronies, walk over to where I was seated, place his hand on my shoulder and demand loudly to see proof that I was old enough to drink.

The bartender interrupted and assured him that I was old enough to be there. The truck driver ignored him.

"I don't drink with kids," he persisted. "Get the hell outta here!"

Before I could respond, Bill told the man to back off and also affirmed that I was old enough to have a drink, adding that I was a Vietnam veteran.

"Vietnam, my ass," the man replied.

His face red, Bill started to turn on his bar stool.

Quickly, with a shake of the head, I signaled my brother not to interfere. "How about I buy you a drink?" I gently offered the truck driver.

He laughed belligerently, reached past me and stuck two of his fingers into my beer glass.

I turned on my stool and faced him squarely.

"Take it outside," the bartender interceded.

"Yeah," the man told me, "outside, *punk*!"

"I'd much rather buy you a beer," I suggested again.

"Outside," he ordered, "or I'm gonna whip your ass right here!"

At that, I punched him in the nose. His body reeled, and he went down on one knee. The bar went silent. The truck driver's nose was bleeding heavily. As he tried to stand, I hit him a second time—much harder than the first—and he fell backward, landing on the seat of his pants. He sat motionless for a second, then toppled over onto his side.

My brother squeezed my forearm and whispered, "Let's get out of here."

As we drove away, Bill said, "You talk so quiet, and then—damn!— all of a sudden, you smack somebody. I was surprised when you popped that guy. I really thought you were going to buy him a drink."

"I *was* going to buy him a drink," I replied. *Why won't people let me live in peace?* I wondered. My patience was wearing thin.

ANDY, MY MOTHER'S DOG, climbed beside me on the couch as I sat there, pondering what to do next. I scratched behind his ears, and he growled lightly in approval. I thought about the several letters I had written to my buddies still in Vietnam. I had flat-out lied to them about how much I enjoyed being free, being *out*—which, I knew, was exactly what they wanted to read.

But the truth is, I'm not fitting in.

The ubiquitous news reports about anti-war protests were like a worsening toothache. What's more, I was starting to regret that I had decided not to return to California. I had no real plans in New York, and it was beginning to look like I would be swinging from job to job. Worse, my social life was dismal. I had looked up some old friends, but—with one or two exceptions—the bonds had dissolved. I had become briefly involved with a young woman who'd written to me after reading "Just What Is Vietnam?" in the *Daily Argus,* and then that ship sank. I also had dated two girls I'd known years before, but my bristling anger chilled their interest. Likewise, my growing and obvious resentment was rapidly reducing my career possibilities.

If I have to go through this personnel interview thing again, maybe I should tell them I traveled the last couple of years, make up stuff and say I'm ready to settle down. Maybe if I don't admit I'm a Vietnam veteran . . .

My face flushed. I was furious at myself. *I'm not going to deny my service, ever,* I declared. I had found a line that I would not cross, and I felt relieved.

As I sat in my mother's living room, I asked myself, "What's *really* bothering me?"

I'm hurt and I'm angry and I'm embarrassed that I lost a job, and I also don't like what's going on in my country.

"What else?"

I sat quietly for several minutes, my mind on hold. There *was* something more, something I couldn't quite reach, something deeper—something that refused to stay buried. Finally, it surfaced:

I had promised not to look for Albert Dorfman, and there's no way I'll break my word to my mother. So why can't I let this go? And why am I suddenly so curious about being a Jew? What difference does it make anyway?

"The thing is, it *is* important to me," I admitted to myself. "Really important, and I don't know why."

It was as if my admission collapsed a barricade. My thoughts began to fall into order, and I made four pledges to myself: First, I'd do whatever was necessary, short of lying about my service, to land another job. At the same time, I would find out how to become a writer. Second, unless a provocation was impossible to circumvent, I'd keep my mouth shut and my hands down. Third, until I got my head straight, I vowed to avoid serious relationships with women. Fourth, I would try to meet more Jewish people, to try to understand where I came from.

OK, where do I begin?

A FEW HOURS LATER, I had a plan. The agent who sold me car insurance had volunteered that I might make a good salesman. And, I remembered, he had encouraged me to phone him for advice. When I called that afternoon, he sounded delighted and asked me to come to his office. Little did I know that I was about to meet someone who would change my life.

CHAPTER 20

THREE DAYS AFTER I lost the job at Nevis Laboratories, David Goldstein hired me as a sales trainee at Metropolitan Life Insurance Company in Manhattan. And since this unusually warm and sensitive man happened to be Jewish, I already had kept *two* of my four pledges.

Over the next few weeks, I also managed to avoid further confrontations (a third pledge kept!), and I began to read seriously about writing, particularly journalism. Then, one night, I came upon an astonishing storyteller who deepened my desire—my *need*—to write:

I sat enthralled as I watched Hal Holbrook perform in *Mark Twain Tonight*. I had never attended a Broadway play before, but I had read several of Twain's books, including *The Adventures of Huckleberry Finn* twice. A friend had asked me to go with him to Holbrook's one-man show after his date had canceled. Although we had low-priced tickets and were seated far to the rear, I felt as if Mark Twain were talking to *me*, and the rest of the audience had been allowed to listen in. I was exhilarated.

I'm going to write, I vowed, and I was never more determined to keep a promise I had made to myself.

But it wasn't long before I broke one of my four pledges—the one about avoiding serious relationships with women. In fact, less than six weeks after I started to work at Metropolitan Life, I asked Loretta Gritz of the Bronx to marry me, and she said "yes."

David Goldstein had introduced the two of us, and when he observed that I didn't seem to be showing enough interest in his lovely assistant, he ordered me to drive Loretta home one day after work. From that afternoon, we were inseparable. It was as if we had known each other for years.

She was tall and slender and beautiful, I thought, with her large brown eyes and light-brown hair and a voice that was as deep and throaty as New York itself. She laughed easily and often. But what made Loretta stand out among other attractive women, at least for me, was her empathy, her simple kindness. It was most evident in small gestures—how easily, for example, she responded when she met someone with an apparent physical handicap or vulnerability.

I remember the night we were seated side by side on a bus, Loretta on the aisle, when a blind man boarded. As he began ambling slowly toward the rear, the bus lurched from the curb, and the man stumbled slightly. Some of the other passengers cast furtive glances while others shifted uneasily, but none moved to help. Loretta, though, stood quickly and clasped the man's forearm, guiding him to an empty seat.

But I didn't discover the basis for Loretta's empathy and kindness until she brought me home to meet her parents for the first time.

At one point, her mother turned away from me—rudely, I thought—as we spoke. "What's wrong with your mother?" I later asked Loretta. "What did I say?"

"Walter," she replied gently, "you didn't say anything wrong. I forgot to tell you that both of my parents are deaf. Just be sure that my mother and father can see you speak. They'll read your lips."

There was no problem understanding *my* mother's feelings: She liked Loretta immediately—and she liked her even more after I announced that we were engaged.

"She's good for you," my mother volunteered.

"Yes, she is," I agreed. Then I added, "Mom, I want to tell her about Albert Dorfman."

She paused only briefly and began to nod.

"I understand," she said. "You shouldn't start your marriage hiding that from your wife. She loves you so much, Walter. She'll be fine with it. If you would just ask her to keep it to herself."

ONE JUNE EVENING in 1966, as we sat in a car parked on Lurting Avenue in the Bronx, Loretta listened patiently while I described my ambition to become a writer. I was acutely aware, though, that she already had come to know a number of people who didn't do what they said they were going to do. I could feel her unspoken doubt—but I also was certain that she wanted me to succeed.

"How are you going to do it?" she asked.

"I haven't figured that out yet," I admitted.

We were quiet for a while, and then I raised a particularly sensitive topic, a question the two of us had yet to resolve. I knew that it was important for Loretta, who'd had a Catholic education, to be married in a Catholic church, specifically St. Lucy's in the Bronx. In order for us to be married in St. Lucy's, however, I—a non-Catholic—would have to give my word to a priest that we would raise our children as Roman Catholics. I could not make such a declaration lightly. I explained to Loretta that I had the same reservations about Catholicism as I'd had

with the Lutheran Church years earlier, when I refused to be confirmed. Nevertheless, I told her, I had decided that I would give my
word.

"Why?" Loretta asked.

"Because," I said, "I trust you. I know that you are a kind and caring
person, and I'd be happy if my children grew up to be just like you. I'll
say it again: *I trust you*. That's a big deal for me."

"Thank you," she said, squeezing my hand.

"Now there's something else . . . ," I began.

"What's that?" she asked.

I spoke for about a half hour, describing my mother's romance, the
tough decisions she had made and, finally, what the story meant to me.

"Walter," said Loretta, "I'm surprised but I'm not surprised. You're
so different from Carol and Billy. And from what I've heard about your
father—about Carol and Billy's father, that is—in a way I'm relieved. I
don't understand why the Jewish part is so important to you, though.
What difference does that make?"

"I don't know," I replied, "but somehow it *is* important to me. I have
feelings about being a Jew that I can't describe. Maybe someday I'll figure it out."

"Should I say something to your mother about knowing her secret?"

I laughed. "I'm sure my mother's waiting to talk to you right now,"
I said. "And, believe me, she'll bring it up as soon as you two are
alone."

Which, of course, my mother did—and Loretta assured her that she
too would keep the promise that I had made: Billy and Carol would
never know.

CHAPTER 21

I SAT BOARD-STRAIGHT in a chair facing the desk of the editor of the *Reporter Dispatch*, a local daily newspaper in White Plains, New York.

William I. Bookman was a slender man, no taller than five feet four, with a smooth pink face and brown eyes that fell into laugh lines behind his glasses. His voice was as gentle as his manner—sincere and friendly, yet confident. Trying to conceal my nervousness, I waited as he quietly studied the two typewritten pages I had handed to him: my résumé.

It was March 1967. I had been working at Metropolitan Life for about ten months before the interview with the *Reporter Dispatch*. Although the people at Metropolitan were supportive, I was an erratic salesman. I knew that selling insurance policies was not for me. This newspaper offered the opportunity I desperately was seeking.

Mr. Bookman finally looked up from the typed pages. "Why do you want to be a reporter?" he asked.

"Because," I answered, "I've wanted to write for as long as I can remember. It is *all* I want to do. If you give me a chance, Mr. Bookman, I won't disappoint you. I earn nearly two hundred dollars a week at Metropolitan, but I'd be willing to work at your newspaper for bus fare. Give me the opportunity to prove myself or to fail. Two weeks. If, after two weeks, you feel I can't be a good reporter, I'll quietly leave."

"Most of the people who work here are college graduates," he said. "Have you ever taken a journalism course?"

"No, sir," I replied. "I have not."

"But you still think you can be a reporter?"

"Yes, I do."

"Why?"

"Mr. Bookman," I asked, "what are the differences between someone you promote and someone you fire?"

He mentioned integrity, curiosity, sensitivity, clarity, desire, drive and persistence, enthusiasm and self-confidence.

"Never once," I pointed out, "have you mentioned a college degree. None of what you've told me can be printed as courses in a university catalog."

He smiled. "Where would you expect to find stories?" he asked. "What are people interested in?"

"Mr. Bookman," I said, "there are stories in every structure on every block in this or any other city. People are interested in people. Families, lives, struggles, joy, sadness, triumph and tragedy, trying and tripping—it's all there if we open our eyes to it."

Aware that my voice was rising and that I was gesticulating, I stopped speaking. I could feel my face redden.

"No, keep going," he suggested.

"It's just that I see these stories around me every day," I said, my voice calm again, "and I'd like to write about them."

"Have you ever been published?" he asked.

"Just a letter I wrote when I was in Vietnam."

"Can I read it?"

I reached into my pocket, withdrew the newspaper clipping and handed it to him across the desk. I waited in silence, the anxiety rising. *Had I made a mistake? Why did I mention it? What if he doesn't like it?*

Finally he nodded.

"That's *very* good," he said.

THREE DAYS LATER, William I. Bookman, who had been an Army sergeant during World War II, called to offer me a job as a reporter with his newspaper at ninety dollars a week. I would have accepted much less. My flesh tingled, my eyes filled, my smile was involuntary.

"Think about it for a couple of days," he suggested.

"I don't have to," I exclaimed. "Yes!"

"Well, then," he replied, his chuckle distinct over the telephone lines, "welcome aboard."

"Mr. Bookman," I said, "thank you."

I HAD BEEN INSTRUCTED to report for work at 7:00 P.M. and ask for the night city editor, a fellow named Larry Smith. It was just 6:15 P.M. as I looked up anxiously at the second-floor windows.

I remembered how boldly I had spoken to Loretta only hours earlier when she said, "It's amazing! How on earth can you just show up to be a reporter?" I told her, "Desire. I want this badly. I'll make it work."

Now, though, faced with the opportunity, I worried: *What if I fail?*

I looked at my watch again. It was still 6:15. I lowered my head and started to walk back toward the parking lot. Then, before I could change my mind, I turned around, crossed the street and pushed open the door to the *Reporter Dispatch*.

Larry Smith arrived about 6:50. I had expected the night city editor to be a silver-haired newspaperman wearing rumpled clothes and a green eyeshade. Instead, to my surprise, he was only a couple of years older than I and wearing a black vest over a neatly pressed white shirt. He gave me my first assignment, which was to attend a meeting of the local beautification committee and to report back to him.

I returned three hours later with enough notes to fill a small book— more than enough to overwhelm and confuse me. Larry, a sincere and serious teacher, sat beside me for an hour and patiently taught me how to ferret out the few facts that I would need to write a brief report.

My first story was only a couple of paragraphs deep inside the *Reporter Dispatch* the next day. Though it didn't contain my byline, I remember touching the newspaper page and running my finger across the story as if it were alive. I *loved* the inky smell, the texture of the newsprint, the words themselves. It was as if a shade had been raised in a darkened room, and I could see.

BY THE TIME I was twenty-two, there already had been four shining dawns in my life: when I was born, when I joined the Marines, when my mother told me about my real father, and when I walked into the *Reporter Dispatch* building on that spring evening in 1967. I could not have imagined what would follow. I knew only that I was compelled by my desire to write. I could no more explain this obsession than I could reach out and clutch the air I breathed.

During my childhood on Eleventh Avenue, Mrs. Williams had sown the seeds that would become my passions to communicate, to learn and to teach. Later, the drill instructors on the broiling sands of Parris Island had encouraged my willingness to lead. In time, these forces would meld and propel me into the future with unexpected velocity. Overcoming painful self-doubt and feelings of inferiority, I would find fulfillment and some success in my field at a relatively young age. In those early months and years, however, I was driven more by a fear of failure than by a yearning for accomplishment.

I was like a runner racing full-tilt on an unfamiliar trail to an unidentified finish line: *Where am I going?* I wondered. *I don't know—but I'd better not slow down.* As a child, I had been defiant. As an adult, I was relentless.

I remember one evening when the rain soaked my hair and dripped down my neck as I struggled to place a jack under the front bumper of my 1965 Pontiac. It was a steamy August night in 1967 along Pines Bridge Road, a shortcut in Mount Kisco, New York. I had covered a school board meeting in a nearby town for the *Reporter Dispatch* and had been returning to the newspaper's office to write the story when a tire blew out.

The meeting had run late—too late for me to call Loretta, as I had promised. We'd be married in a couple of weeks, and I had bought a hundred-dollar suit on credit, a considerable investment for someone earning ninety dollars a week. That night, as I wore the suit for the first time, mud spattered above my cuffs, and my shoes squished as I walked to the rear of the car to return the jack. As I opened the trunk lid, a car passed too closely. It hit a deep puddle and sent a thick, muddy shower over me.

"Hey, stop!" I yelled, shaking my fist at the two red taillights as they grew smaller and finally disappeared into the darkness.

With the rain beating the pavement about me, I dropped my hand, which was skinned and bleeding from the lug wrench, and lowered my head. What else could go wrong? My new suit, its blue wool wrinkled and soaked from top to bottom, clung to my skin.

I thought about the calculations Loretta and I had made the night before. Together, before deductions, we would earn about one hundred and eighty dollars a week, but our monthly payments for necessities would exceed what we would actually take home by seven dollars. I had three choices: I could forget writing and seek a higher-paying job in another field, I could find a second job to supplement our income, or I could go to school while I worked as a reporter and apply for veterans' tuition assistance. Although the executives at the *Reporter Dispatch* encouraged me to further my education, they made it clear that I could expect no help. The newspaper had no tuition-reimbursement program. If I wanted a degree, I'd have to pay for it on my own. The benefit for Vietnam veterans was less than it had been for those who served in World War II or Korea. Still, at nearly fifty dollars a month for part-time students, it meant that—if I enrolled at Westchester Community College, the area's least-expensive school—we could survive as long as I passed the courses I had been assigned. Could I?

As I listened to the only sound in the air—the steady rain—my spirits withered. *How can I work a full-time job and complete college? How can I possibly marry Loretta? I'm going to fail,* I told myself, finally allowing the dark curtain of doubt to extinguish my last fragment of will.

I trembled. Minutes passed. Then, somewhere in my gloom, I remembered myself as a small boy on a stoop—a boy who had looked into the night and promised, *I'm getting out of here.* I raised my head slowly in the rain and whispered, "I am not quitting."

CHAPTER 22

I

T WAS AN AUGUST MORNING in 1970 when Andrew G. Nelson, the director of admissions at Mercy College in Dobbs Ferry, New York, asked me why I had enrolled for a single course at his school.

"Because," I explained, "I can't afford more. My wife is only weeks away from having our first child. She can't work any longer, and the tuition at Mercy—though less than the other four-year schools in the area—is still more than twice what I was paying at Westchester Community College. One course is the best I can do."

"Have you applied for any scholarships?" he asked.

"No," I replied.

He looked down again at my transcript, a single sheet of paper. It reported the courses I had completed and the grades I had received to obtain an associate of arts degree in liberal arts and social sciences the previous June from Westchester Community College.

"You graduated first among six hundred and two graduates?" he asked, not looking up.

"Actually, I was one of two valedictorians," I said. "Another student and I had identical grade-point averages—one B . . ."

"And all the rest A's," he finished.

"Yes," I said.

I studied my watch. I hadn't expected an interview. I just wanted to register for one course and return to work, and I felt rushed.

"Mr. Nelson," I asked, "is there a problem?"

"No," he said, "but I wish you had applied for a scholarship last spring. You might have received some assistance."

"Thank you for the encouragement," I replied. "But I'm going to be twenty-six in a couple of days, I only decided to pursue a bachelor's degree in the last few weeks, and I'm trying to register *before* I change my mind."

"I have a few questions," he told me.

Andrew G. Nelson was about my age. He gesticulated vigorously, almost rocking in his chair, and his tone reflected his exuberance. It was his enthusiasm that made me curious and kept me seated when, in fact, I should have been elsewhere.

I asked to use his phone and called my office to say that I'd been detained. Then I sat back and said, "Ask away, Mr. Nelson."

"Call me Andy," he offered.

"Andy," I said, "what do you want to know?"

"Would you take more courses at Mercy College if you could afford to?"

I paused. I had worked full-time while attending Westchester Community College. Did I really want to do that again? Two *more* years of studying every weekend and nearly every night? How would my wife—soon to become a mother and no longer bringing home a pay-check—respond?

"Probably," I replied.

"Would you continue in the social sciences?" he asked.

"Yes," I said, "I'd major in psychology."

"Not English or journalism?"

"No," I said.

"Why not?" he asked.

"While I was in the Marine Corps," I explained, "I read more novels and more nonfiction by more authors than I could ever expect to be assigned in college. I started out as a local reporter for the *Reporter Dispatch*, and a year later I was appointed night city editor. Today, as the editor of *HELP!*, the action line I started for the newspapers in Westchester County, my columns appear not only in the *Reporter Dispatch* but in seven other daily newspapers as well, and they draw nearly five hundred letters a week. Andy, I *am* a journalist. I write every day. If I concentrate my studies in English or take a lot of writing courses, I'll learn much less than if I major in the social sciences."

Andy Nelson made a note on a small scratch pad, rose from his seat, shook my hand and announced, "Welcome to Mercy College, Walter."

The following day, he called me at the newspaper and asked if I could stop by the college.

"It was too late to register after all, wasn't it?" I said, squeezing the telephone tightly.

"No," he said, chuckling. "I have some good news for you. You have a scholarship . . ."

"What?" I interrupted.

"A complete academic scholarship," he finished. "I showed your transcript to the president, Pat Coogan, and she awarded you the full scholarship. No strings. Just continue to get good grades. You have to stop by today, though, to register full-time. Can you do it?"

"Yes," I told him. Then I quickly called Loretta.

"That's wonderful!" she said when I told her the news. "And it was very generous of Mercy College."

"I know," I agreed. "But keep in mind that I'll be working full-time and attending college full-time all over again for another two years."

"You'll do fine," she replied. "And *we'll* do fine, baby and all."

I paused. "I have just one regret."

"Really?"

"Yes," I said. "I wish Mrs. Williams could see how I'm doing now."

OUR SON, ERIC, was born a couple of weeks later, on September 17, at Albert Einstein College of Medicine in the Bronx. I looked at his tiny body in the bassinet, and suddenly I was consumed by my responsibility as his father. *How do I protect you?* I wondered.

Loretta, who was as uncertain as I was, suggested that we seek advice on how to be good parents from someone we trusted—Dr. Adma d'Heurle, my psychology mentor at Mercy College.

"The most important lesson Eric will learn," she counseled, "is to trust. It will be the base you can build upon in the years to come." She also said we must show unconditional love to our son and discipline him gently—and only when absolutely necessary—during his first year. Clearly, if Loretta and I succeeded, Eric's boyhood would be different from my own.

MY MOTHER ALSO had someone new in her life. She had met and married a retired restaurateur named Gene D'Ambra shortly before Eric was born, and she was elated. Her new husband, an attentive and articulate gentleman, could not have been more different from the man who had raised me. Gene had been widowed a couple of years before and had no children of his own, so Eric's birth took on a special meaning for him. My mother also had shared with Gene the truth about my real father and, of course, asked him to keep it a secret from Billy and Carol, which he promised to do.

After seeing Eric for the first time in the hospital, my mother drew me aside and asked, "Is he circumcised?"

"Of course," I said, and we both laughed.

CHAPTER 23

I SQUEEZED THE STEERING WHEEL TIGHTLY. My passenger, the editor of *New York* magazine, had just asked me to accept an assignment. Clay Felker was a world-renowned journalist who, at forty-three, was at the top of his profession. And yet I was about to decline his offer.

"I don't know," I said. "To tell you the truth, as much as I'd like to write for you, Mr. Felker, I don't want to go back to the street. I've invested several months of my life exposing heroin sales and the black market in methadone and, frankly, I'm sick of it. I don't want to write about drugs again."

Less than a year earlier, shortly after I had started my studies at Mercy College, I had been promoted to chief investigative reporter for the Westchester Rockland Newspapers. Some of my work had been picked up by the Associated Press and thus received wider attention.

"I'm not asking you to start all over again, Walter," he said. "I'm interested in how you did the investigation."

"*How* I did it?"

"Yes," he said, "precisely what did you do on the street to get the information you published?"

I stopped the car but left the engine running. It was a Thursday night in the dead of winter, 1972. Clay Felker had been the featured speaker earlier that evening at a meeting of journalists in Westchester County, and I had been asked to drive this legendary figure back to Manhattan.

"What did I do on the street?" I repeated.

"Yes," he said. "Your editor told me about the results—how you proved the country's first death by methadone, how your stories prompted mass arrests of heroin dealers and so on. But I'm willing to bet *how* you did the investigation is the most interesting story of all."

"Mr. Felker," I replied, "I received some of the most valuable information from street people—addicts, muggers, burglars and prostitutes. The criminal records of some of my sources run on page after page. Do you still want me to write about this?"

"Very much," he said, his tone even and sincere. "I want you to tell it as it happened."

Sold by his enthusiasm, I agreed to do the story and to have it on his desk the first thing Monday morning.

When we arrived at his address, Felker shook my hand and stepped out of the car. But before leaving, he turned and asked, "By the way, Walt, why were you able to talk so easily to those street people?"

I laughed. "I used to live there," I said. Then I drove away and headed home.

Three nights later, staring at the blank page I had inserted in my portable typewriter, I remembered Clay Felker's instruction: "I want you to tell it as it happened."

Easier said than done, I thought. My deadline was the next morning.

I had written several false starts, but each read like the newspaper articles I already had published. Finally, frustrated, I stood up.

"Where are you going?" Loretta asked as she rocked Eric, who was
almost a year and a half old.

"I'm having trouble writing the *New York* piece," I said. "I don't
know where or how to start it, and I wish I'd never agreed to it. Clay
Felker is crazy. I'm going for a walk."

We were then living on the third floor of a three-family house in the
northeast Bronx. I slipped into a coat, walked down the stairs to the
street and stepped into the chill air.

As I walked, it was as if I were traveling in someone else's body: I
was oblivious to everything but my own thoughts. I must have passed
storefronts, corner drugstores and bars, the subway and the housing
projects, but I was aware of none of those things. I kept asking myself,
How do I begin? How do I begin? But the more I strained to think, the
more difficult it became, until I finally told myself, *I'm just not good
enough. I'll call Clay Felker in the morning and tell him I can't do the piece.*

Suddenly, as if a movie had just flashed on a screen and startled me,
I became aware of where I was: seven blocks from home. For the first
time since I'd started out, I also became aware of others—an old
woman walking slowly with a cane, two teenagers moving briskly, a
couple laughing as they entered a corner bar.

I turned back, and then, close to home, it came to me: *That's it! People! The story is about the people I know!*

I bounded up the three flights to our apartment two steps at a time,
opened the door and heard Loretta say, "You've got it!"

"How can you tell?" I asked.

"You're smiling," she said.

As I sat down to write, once again I heard Clay Felker's words: "I
want you to tell it as it happened."

I began typing, describing in detail some of the characters I had met.
I recalled my research findings, my interviews with doctors and with

police. I discussed the autopsies I had viewed to gain a better under-standing of drug abuse and how the Westchester medical examiner's forensic findings helped me to prove what was believed to be the nation's first methadone death, one of nine that I discovered.

I finished typing early Monday morning and told Loretta I was tak-ing the subway to Manhattan to turn the story in.

"Then what?" she asked.

"Then," I said, "we pray they accept it."

WITH MY FELLOW STUDENTS applauding, my throat seemed to thicken, and I struggled not to cry. As I stepped down from the podium, I saw Loretta trying to squeeze her arms through the lines of people to take my picture. It was the June 1972 commencement at Mercy College, and I had just received the gold medal for psychology. As valedictorian of the graduating class, I also had been awarded the college president's Medal for Preeminent Scholarship.

When I reached my seat, a fellow student—a mother in her forties who had taken all her courses at night—pinched me on the arm and said, "You did good, kid!" My eyes filled.

Across the crowds, over the heads of students and well-wishers, I spotted my wife again. We both smiled. I knew that Loretta, more than any other person, understood what it had taken to achieve that moment. She had shared it all—the scrimping, the strain, the loss of evenings and weekends.

She nodded.

I nodded back.

How much my life is changing, I thought. *I'm just twenty-seven. Maybe it's changing too fast.* In the fall, I would be teaching psychology and sociology courses at night as an adjunct professor at Westchester Com-munity College. And that was in addition to my newspaper work.

Westchester Rockland Newspapers was going to give me the chance to be managing editor of its news bureau in Westchester County. If I succeeded, I could end up as the editor of a newspaper. On top of that, the methadone piece had been a success, and earlier that week Clay Felker had asked me to do more investigative work for his magazine. He'd also encouraged me to become an editor. *I should be happy*, I thought, *but I'm nervous. Am I good enough?*

Then, gazing out at the rows of other students receiving their degrees under the large tent at Mercy College, I told myself that I would worry tomorrow, not today.

ON A BRISK SUNDAY MORNING about eighteen months after the Mercy College graduation, I pulled into a metered parking space near the corner of North Avenue and Huguenot Street in New Rochelle. It was in the late fall of 1973. As I looked through the car window at the two-story concrete block building across the street, I considered the irony.

That narrow building held the offices of an 18,000-circulation newspaper, the *Standard-Star*. Next door was the post office where I had met the gunnery sergeant who recruited me into the Marine Corps more than twelve years earlier. I remembered how nervous I had been when I signed the papers that day. I was just sixteen. In my mind now, I watched the boy I had been then: I saw young Walter leaving that post office, both thrilled and frightened, then turning back after a few steps to stare again at the Marine recruiting poster. I seemed to stand a little taller than before I'd signed up, and my chin jutted out as I walked away. Then I tripped at the curb, which ended my swagger and sent blood to my neck and cheeks.

I laughed at the memory, then looked again at the *Standard-Star*. In a few weeks, I would be the editor and general manager of this daily newspaper. *Anderson*, I wondered, *are you going to trip again?*

"Elmer Miller is retiring," Thomas P. Dolan, the president and publisher of the Westchester Rockland Newspapers, had told me. "I want you to succeed him as editor and general manager in New Rochelle. You'll run the whole paper, do both jobs. I know you can do it."

I had been managing editor at headquarters for more than a year. Now, at twenty-nine, I would be the youngest general manager and one of the youngest editors in the newspaper group. I exuded confidence when I spoke with Tom Dolan, but inside I was as unsure as that sixteen-year-old boy.

CHAPTER 24

As I stood at the edge of my sister's grave, the minister's words rolled by me. I remembered not the woman he described but a blond girl who tattled to our father about something I had done after I had tattled on her. I remembered how, afterward, we had made a pact: Neither of us would divulge secrets about the other—and, throughout our lives, we never did. I remembered the Rockettes, a group of teenage girls who had named themselves after the famous Radio City Music Hall dancers, how they wore satin jackets to high school and how they were led by my sister, one of the tiniest in the group. I remembered my sister's fight with a much larger girl who had accused her of bleaching her hair. That girl had ended up running home with a bloody nose and a torn blouse.

I looked across the mourners assembled that September morning in

1974 toward our big brother Bill. He was always larger than life to Carol and me—a fighter, a motorcycle racer—always, it seemed, an experience ahead of each of us. His memories, I knew, would be different from mine: Carol was his little sister; she was my big sister. I watched my mother standing quietly, and I understood that I could not comprehend her pain; I could only suffer *with* her. We had lost a sister, but she had lost a daughter. Carol's husband had lost a wife. Her three children and a foster child had lost their mother. How differently we'd all remember the small blond lady with the large blue eyes.

I had saved the two letters she wrote to me when I was in Vietnam:

September 21, 1965

I've been thinking about you all the time. I just finished watching the news on television. I hope you take care of yourself. We all love you and we want you home safely. The kids are in school now . . . so I have some peace and quiet. Daddy comes up here more and he talks about you a lot. Even though he doesn't say it to you, he's proud of you. I will write soon. I love you, little brother. Please be careful.

Love, Carol

November 21, 1965

I pray every day that you are safe. You're my little brother, you know. Mommy called me up to tell me your picture and your letter were in the Daily Argus. *She read it to me. It's hard to describe how I felt. It was perfect the way you put it, Walter. Not even a writer could do it better. I'm so proud of you. When you get out of the Marines, I hope you go to college in New York State. I don't want you to move far away. You've been away from all of us so long already. Please be careful.*

Love, Carol

P.S. I weigh 105 pounds!

I remembered how, during a posh political fund-raising party at the White Plains Hotel two years earlier, my sister—who was then a sub-urban housewife and a district leader from northern Westchester County—held my arm tightly and asked, "What do you think all these people would say if they knew where we came from?"

"They'd ask you for your autograph, sweetheart," I told her.

"I'll bet," she said.

"Would you like me to introduce you as the former leader of the Rockettes?" I asked.

"I'll break your neck," she told me and pinched my forearm.

I remembered my sister in a hospital bed, her ovaries and a breast removed, a doctor confiding that she might live only a few months. Cancer, he said, was killing her. I remembered, more than a year later, how Carol and I had talked in the living room of her home.

"I don't know about this chemotherapy," she said. "It makes me sick."

"Are you going to let them operate again?" I asked.

"No," she said. "What I have left is what I'm going to die with. I'm not going to let them bury me in pieces."

"Why do you pretend with almost everyone that you don't know what's happening to you?" I asked.

"That I'm dying?"

"Yes," I said.

"Because," she replied, "it's easier on them. I have only one regret, and I can't do anything about it."

"What's that?"

"I'll never see my children become adults."

I touched her hand. We were quiet for a couple of minutes, and then I reminded her how she had held my daughter, Melinda, born that June. "I'm glad you saw Melinda," I said.

How badly I wanted to confide to Carol the one secret that I had kept from her, but I could not break my vow to our mother. *I know you would understand*, I thought.

"Carol," I told her, "I love you."

"I know that," she said. "I've always known that. I love you too, little brother."

CHAPTER 25

I SAW A FAMILIAR FACE across the wide, brightly lighted newsroom—the modern home of the *Reporter Dispatch* in Harrison,
New York—but I approached him slowly, quietly. I wanted the
moment to matter. No longer were there the ragtag rows of splintered,
stained wooden desks that I remembered. No pneumatic tubes overhead
that whisked stories to Teletype setters; no boiling lead cooled and
punched, letter by letter, into type; no familiar, moist odor of ink that
seemed forever to pervade the old *Reporter Dispatch* building in White
Plains. No, it was now 1975, and there were shiny metal desks firmly
planted in precise rows and little screens with typewriter keyboards.
There was even carpeting!

I laughed to myself, recalling how a city hall reporter had once dusted
off his desk with his tie at the old building and then remarked, "I wanted to see what would float up into the air." And how a female reporter

had stripped off her blouse on a hot summer day when the temperature inside reached the temperature outside. *No, that wouldn't happen here*, I thought as I looked around this modern newsroom. I knew that a mammoth computer hummed somewhere in this glass-and-concrete structure, operated by people called programmers who electronically translated the reporters' messages into long, even paper columns that later were sided with hot wax, cut and pasted, then formed into the pages that were published daily.

The man I had come to see was studying a sheet of typed notes as I stepped carefully into his office. His back was turned to me, and I did not want to disturb him—not yet—for these seconds were precious to me. Once he had been the editor of a newspaper, but now he was an editorial writer and a columnist. I noticed that his hair had silvered more, and he wore stylish metal-frame glasses that rode higher on his nose. Still, I recognized him. I'd always recognize him. His name was Bill Bookman, and he'd given me my first opportunity as a journalist eight years earlier, when I was a high school dropout.

"Would you like me to edit that for you?" I asked.

Startled, he turned, smiled widely and then said, "I guess you're looking for a job."

We both laughed.

The reunion was warm and genuine. A few minutes later, as we reminisced, I noticed that some reporters and editors were gathering across the newsroom, outside my new office.

"Bill," I said, nodding toward the group, "I'm about to be introduced to these people, and many of them, I'm sure, would rather lynch me."

"Why?"

"They're not my team, Bill," I said. "To them, I'm the outsider. My predecessor assembled that crew. I only know a few of them."

"You'll do fine," he reassured me, pointing out the experience I had gained during the last year as editor and general manager of the *Standard-Star*. "They need you here, Walter."

"I hope you're right," I replied as I stepped out of his office. I could feel my pulse rising as I took my first step across the newsroom of the 50,000-circulation newspaper. The moment to reflect, the joy of reunion, was over. I had just become the fourth editor in only a few years of what had been candidly described to me as "a demoralized newspaper," one that had undergone considerable turmoil among its staff.

Many reporters and editors, I knew, distrusted me. I was acutely aware that critics described me as overbearing, blindly ambitious, impetuous and argumentative. Unfortunately, I had earned every criticism. It was not my competence that critics questioned, but my personality. I was prickly. On the one hand, reporters and editors seemed to respect my creative abilities, my willingness to lead and my enthusiasm. On the other hand, my failure to gracefully accept criticism—and my temper—turned them off. My professional and educational successes should have made me more congenial, more confident, but instead I was still haunted by feelings of inferiority. I agonized silently—irrationally—that somehow, inexplicably, I'd lose everything that I'd gained. I was thirty years old, and I was still angry.

CHAPTER 26

I WAS AN HOUR EARLY for my luncheon appointment at the Marco Polo Club in the Waldorf-Astoria. *Good*, I thought, *more time to think*. I started to walk uptown along Park Avenue, past the famous hotel. What, I wondered, would Jess Gorkin ask me this time? I was one of the three final candidates that an executive recruiter had recommended for a senior editor's position at *Parade* magazine, the Sunday supplement that appeared in newspapers throughout the country, and I was sure my rivals were more qualified. Perhaps, I worried, I shouldn't have been so candid in my written review of his publication. After all, Jess Gorkin had been the editor of *Parade* for three decades. Who was I to evaluate his work, even if he had asked? We'd met twice before, and I had decided that—for better or worse—I'd be myself. Privately, though, I wished I had more to offer. My work seemed so anemic. *Parade* was a magazine, and my experience, except for an article here and there, was purely in news-papering.

It was a sunny May day in 1977, an exceptional afternoon to enjoy Manhattan. For all I noticed, though, it could have been snowing. The more I concentrated and practiced what I *might* say, the more doubts I raised. Block after block, my anxiety grew, and I had no sense that I had traveled nearly a mile when I looked at my watch. There was no time to walk back! Fortunately, I was able to flag a cab and make it to the Wal-dorf with a couple of minutes to spare.

Jess Gorkin already had arrived, and I was led to his table.

He spoke gently. I wondered, listening to him, how many people would recognize this slight, bald, unassuming man in the conservative pin-striped suit as the fellow who had persuaded a president of the Unit-ed States, John F. Kennedy, and a Soviet premier, Nikita Khrushchev, to create the famous hot line between their two countries. It was *his* idea, and Jess Gorkin made it happen, just as he later helped to achieve another remarkable piece of diplomacy—the first joint spaceflight involving the Soviet Union and the United States.

Why am I here? I silently wondered. The *Reporter Dispatch* is one thing. *Parade*, with the largest circulation of any publication in America, is quite another.

"I liked your analysis of *Parade*," Jess began after we'd had lunch, "and I particularly liked your ideas. You have a way of seeing through a complicated problem quickly and suggesting a solution." He paused. "But are you aware that you're recommending changing something that's very successful?"

My life had come to this moment. I was thirty-two. I had been a jour-nalist for precisely a decade, and I had learned some important lessons during the last two years as editor and general manager of the *Reporter Dispatch*. Not the least of these lessons was that I had begun to under-stand, despite many failures, how to criticize others without stirring resentment and how to welcome criticism myself. More importantly, after several fits and starts, I was learning to channel my anger—and my fears—to productive ends.

I finally realized that for years I had been running *from* something, and now I was running *toward* a goal: I had found myself inexorably drawn to help expose and relieve social problems such as child abuse, racism and illiteracy, and I discovered that each new opportunity gave me a greater chance to influence the issues I cared most about. I knew that the *Reporter Dispatch* had done well, and my contribution was valued. But I also knew that I could not turn down a once-in-a-lifetime opportunity to be an editor for the most widely read magazine in the United States as well as a chance to learn from a man who had brought nations together.

How should I answer Jess Gorkin's question? If I suggest change, won't I be criticizing his work and destroy any chance I might have of being hired? If, on the other hand, I believe change is called for and I remain silent, what am I? How badly do I want this job?

"Jess," I said, "you're a great editor, and frankly I'm sitting here thinking, 'Who am I to evaluate your work?' Well, you asked, and I guess I'm going to have to wager that you really want me to answer. This is my view . . ."

I spoke for fifteen minutes. Jess didn't interrupt, and his face stayed expressionless. I had no sense of what he felt. I explained what I thought was very good about *Parade* and where I thought improvement was necessary. Some of my comments, I knew, struck at ideas that he had encouraged for years. *In for a penny, in for a pound,* I told myself. *Let him hear it all.* When I finished, I immediately wished that I had said nothing.

He was silent.

Well, that's that, I thought.

"Walter," he said finally, "I do not want to hire you to be a senior editor at *Parade* . . ."

My stomach twisted.

"I want you to be my assistant," he continued, "though you'll have the title of senior editor. Within a year, I will promote you to managing editor. Then, within another year, if everything goes well, you will succeed me."

The salary and benefits he mentioned were more than I had planned to ask for. Now *I* was silent.

"Jess," I said quietly, "will you please excuse me for a moment?"

I rose from my chair, walked to the bathroom, checked the stalls to be sure I was alone, faced the mirror, threw up my hands and said, "All right!"

When I returned to the table, I somehow managed to speak calmly, my voice serious. "That's certainly a generous offer," I told Jess, "and I appreciate it. So that I can discuss this with my employers and give it more thought, may I have a week to give you an answer?"

"Of course, Walter," he told me. His eyes seemed to twinkle, as if he wanted to smile, but he didn't.

After we said goodbye a few minutes later, I ran to a telephone in the Waldorf, misdialed once and then dialed correctly.

"Hello," my wife answered.

"Guess what?" I asked, my voice cracking.

Loretta laughed.

"I think I can," she said.

CHAPTER 27

IT WAS A WARM MORNING early in the summer of 1980, and I sat across the desk from Samuel I. Newhouse Jr. His office was in the Condé Nast Building on Madison Avenue, not far from Grand Central Station.

The Newhouse family owned *Parade* among other interests, including more than twenty daily newspapers, the Random House book publishing company, several cable television systems and Condé Nast, a company that published such stylish magazines as *Vogue, Glamour* and *House & Garden*. This was to be my first meeting with the man who managed this vast, billion-dollar communications company with his younger brother, Donald, and other family members.

It had been three years since my first day at *Parade*. I still could clearly recall how disappointed I was when, just six months after I joined the magazine, Jess Gorkin left *Parade* to become the editor of a new magazine called *Fifty Plus*. I did not succeed Jess. Instead, he was replaced by his managing editor, James D. Head, a journalist who had been my executive editor when I was an investigative reporter with the Westchester Rockland Newspapers. Although Jim Head was a friend and assured me that he would name me managing editor, as Jess Gorkin had promised, I was crushed at the time. I remember the conversation I had with my wife the day after I learned that Jess had been asked to retire by Jim McAllister, the president of the magazine.

"I'm going to quit," I told Loretta.

"Why?" she asked.

"Because I won't be the editor of the magazine," I said. "That's the reason I came to *Parade* in the first place. I have a hundred ideas I'd like to try."

"Walter," she asked, "are you really ready to be editor of *Parade*?"

I didn't answer. I knew I was angrily responding out of hurt.

That night I slept poorly. Finally, at four in the morning, I got out of bed and went into the darkened living room. Sitting alone, the air still, I finally conceded that I was *not* ready. I was not yet equipped to be the editor of a magazine. I had more to learn.

Now, less than three years later, Jim Head had resigned to help start up a children's magazine called *Three To Get Ready*. Carlo Vittorini, the new publisher of *Parade*, and David Starr, the senior editor of Newhouse Newspapers, had recommended to the owners that I be named editor, though I was only thirty-five. And I was in the office of Samuel I. Newhouse Jr., who would make the decision.

The meeting lasted half an hour. He asked me to call him "Si," and he frequently folded his hands before him as he spoke. He had brown eyes, curly black hair and a modest demeanor. I knew that he was fifty-two, but he seemed younger to me, stronger somehow. *Maybe it's his power*, I thought. *No, it was something else.*

He was rumored to be an extremely private person, and Si New-house was indeed a quiet man. But his questions, which he asked softly, were perceptive.

I found myself discussing quality. "The only medium that attracts audiences as large as *Parade* is television," I said. "The success of shows like *Roots*, *60 Minutes* and *Brian's Song* is no accident. Americans demand quality. If we match the right writer with the right idea, our readers will respond."

"Walter," he asked, "whom do you plan to publish?"

"The widest variety of American authors," I said. "People as diverse as Norman Mailer and John Cheever and Gail Sheehy and Herman Wouk and David Halberstam and Irving Wallace and Erica Jong and Alex Haley and Studs Terkel."

"Do you know these writers?" he asked.

"In a sense."

"*In a sense?*" he repeated, clearly curious.

"I've never met any of them," I admitted, "but I know them from their work."

He was silent for several seconds. "Are you confident you can attract these writers to *Parade?*"

"Yes," I said, my enthusiasm bubbling up, "I am. *Parade* will be a receptive environment in which ideas flourish. In other words, it's going to be exciting. No, more than that, it's going to be irresistible. Why will the authors participate? Because the ideas will be compelling, not clever. We'll get their blood rushing. Something else . . ."

"What is that?" he asked.

"I believe," I said, "that if I appeal to their more noble motives, we'll get their finest work."

〜

NOT LONG AFTER Si Newhouse appointed me editor of *Parade* in 1980, my mother observed, "You've been helped by a lot of Jewish people in your career."

"Yes," I agreed, "but I've also been helped by a lot of people who aren't Jewish, Mom."

Her point interested me, though. David Goldstein, Bill Bookman, Clay Felker, Jess Gorkin and Si Newhouse *were* all Jewish—and all went out of their way to give me a chance. What's more, each had genuinely encouraged me. It was reasonable to assume that they all thought I was Catholic or Protestant, if they thought about it at all.

I had been careful over the years—since the day I learned about my real father—to disguise my curiosity about Judaism, but I had read as much as I could, observed others and listened. What intrigued me most was the Jewish emphasis on behavior: An ethical life, I learned, is essential to a Jew. If a Jewish man steals, for example, he may seek forgiveness from God. But if he's to be forgiven, he has to seek forgiveness from the person he harmed, and he must right the wrong. "I'm sorry" is not nearly enough.

By the time I became editor of *Parade*, I had begun to gain a better understanding of what it meant to be Jewish, but I still lacked a depth of feeling. That was about to change.

CHAPTER 28

ONE WINTER EVENING in 1982, I attended a lecture by Elie Wiesel at Lincoln Center in Manhattan. He was a compelling storyteller, and I was enthralled. It was as if I were reliving the day I had finished reading his memoir *Night* as a young Marine— and, once again, I was riveted by his words. But this time I also was riveted by his eyes. Later, when I arrived home, I wrote a note to myself: "If ever eyes revealed a soul, they would be his—*dark* brown eyes, the most distinctive and compelling of any human being I have known." It was clear to me that few photographs captured the depth of his eyes, their sadness, the opaque reflections of the unimaginable tragedies he had witnessed.

Elie had been only fifteen when the Nazis—in what may still have seemed to some of them an inexorable march to glory—finally arrived in his remote hometown, the village of Sighet in the Carpathian Mountains of Romania-Hungary, in 1944. The soldiers, by then chillingly efficient at their murderous business, quickly deported the entire Jewish population. Elie's family first was sent to Auschwitz, where his mother and younger sister were killed. Then he and his father were ordered on to the Buchenwald camp, where his father was starved to death. Elie somehow managed to survive, as did his two older sisters.

When the Allies liberated Buchenwald in 1945, the young survivor vowed to himself not to speak for ten years about the horrors he had seen, and he kept this vow of silence. When, finally, he did speak, he was like a bursting dam. Starting in 1958 with *Night*, Elie Wiesel has written more than forty books, as well as hundreds of essays and articles. He also has given speeches, and they have—as he had hoped— paid eloquent witness to the Holocaust. And he has spoken out for Southeast Asia refugees, South African blacks, the Miskito Indians of Nicaragua, Argentine political prisoners and Soviet Jewry.

After Elie spoke that evening at Lincoln Center, I introduced myself to him as the editor of *Parade*. I also called him the next day. *Night* had affected me profoundly when I read it on a troop ship headed to Vietnam, but I'd had no one to discuss it with at the time. *Now,* I thought, *I'll be able to talk with Elie Wiesel himself!* When we met for lunch a couple of weeks later for what would turn out to be the first of many conversations in the years to come, I was irresistibly drawn to this gentle man. I could not have imagined how close we'd become, how Elie would answer so many of my questions and guide me.

Our conversations, I noticed, often evolved into question-and-answer dialogues, mainly with me asking and Elie replying.

"My greatest fear," he once responded to a question of mine, "has been that what happened during the Holocaust will not be transmitted. I say this knowing that it was the most documented tragedy in history and that never before has such misery been so carefully recorded by so many—by the victims, the killers, the bystanders. The tormentors themselves kept statistics. They had competitions. Murder squads competed to see who killed more. Detailed records were meticulously kept, boasting entries like, 'Ten days; 80,000 Jews.' Yet—in spite of these documents, the books, the pictures, the films, all the testimony, the words of the survivors and the witnesses—still some things remain beyond comprehension."

"Elie," I asked, "how did you survive?"

"By accident. Every day, ten thousand people left the camp. Most were killed; others died on the way. I happened to be in the group of two or three hundred at the gate who were the overflow. The quota was filled. It just happened. Not only could I not plan it, I did not *want* to plan it. I was a boy, and to remain alive without those I loved, those who loved me—well, it did not seem like life as I wanted it."

"Did you believe you were going to die there?" I asked.

"I was convinced I would not survive. I wasn't the type to survive. I was always a weak child. I was sickly, always going to doctors, only interested in study, not sports, always vulnerable."

"At sixteen," I said, "you knew your parents had been killed, yet you ended up doing something positive out of that. How?"

"It wasn't easy. It took many years."

"To overcome anger?"

"Overcome? No, I'm still angry. I am outraged. I am not against anger. I am against hate."

"Why don't you hate those responsible?" I asked.

"It would be silly to reduce such enormous horror, a tragedy unprecedented in the history of man, to hatred. That would be a betrayal of my parents and my friends." He paused. "Because," he continued, speaking slowly, "if I hated, I would betray their deaths. The enemy *wanted* us to hate him. I refuse. I will not grant the killer's wish. In the Bible, the first death is a murder. Cain is slaying his brother, Abel. Is the point of the murder that brothers ultimately must kill each other? Or does the story mean that whoever kills, kills his brother? We're told not to hate our brother in our hearts; hatred inevitably destroys the hater as well as the hated. The choice is ours. I choose to believe that he who kills, kills his brother and, finally, himself. We are responsible for what we are."

"Was there hatred in the camps?"

"Yes," he replied. "In Auschwitz I saw hate. The camp inside was ruled and managed by inmates, and anti-Semitism existed among them too. Some Ukrainians and Poles hated Jews and allowed their frustration and rage to overcome them. I have seen inmates kill inmates. But also I have seen people take risks and remain human. I can tell you I have seen a man take bread and offer it to an unknown inmate. Yet it was dangerous not to eat one's own bread—that was one day less to live. I have seen a man intervene on behalf of someone else. This was not a father-son relationship; they were strangers. Tenderness existed even there among people."

"Why did you wait ten years before speaking about the Holocaust?" I asked.

"I really believe my survival had no meaning. But *because* I survived, I have to give it meaning. For ten years, I was afraid to speak. I was afraid that what I wanted to say I would not be able to say. Truly, the testimony that the survivors have to give cannot be given. The killer's brutality was so extreme as to deprive us of the language to tell of his brutality. The words, I feared, did not exist. That's why I waited ten years, to purify the language in me."

"Are you sure of the words today?"

"They are as close as possible to what I want to say," he replied.

"What," I asked finally, "have you learned to value most?"

"I have learned, because of what I've witnessed, to sanctify life. I cherish life." He paused, seeming to weigh his words even more carefully. "And because I have seen so many children killed, every child is precious to me. When I see a child, I cry inside. I have come to celebrate life—not only mine and yours but also the lives of people whom neither of us will ever come to know. We all work with what we are, Walter. I could have been crushed by events or saved by them."

As this gentle man described his feelings about children, I could not help but reflect on my own childhood, and I found perspective: As painful as my home life may have been, as deeply as I may have at times hated my father, my experience was insignificant compared to what Elie had witnessed. After all, I could leave Eleventh Avenue—and I did. No such choice was possible for Elie or for the children he knew in the camps. Nevertheless, I knew that, despite the stark differences in our experiences, we arrived, finally, at the same place: Every child *is* precious.

IN 1986, FOUR YEARS after we first met, it was announced that Elie Wiesel would receive the Nobel Peace Prize. The Nobel committee described my friend as a messenger to humankind, one of Earth's most important spiritual leaders—a man whose message, they said, was one of peace, atonement and human dignity. I called on the morning of the announcement to congratulate him. I was ecstatic; he was humble. When I placed the telephone down, I was sure that Elie would somehow find a way to use the good news to help others. Thus, I was not surprised when I learned a short time later that he had donated the financial part of his prize to create the Foundation for Humanity, which is dedicated to examining the root causes of social phenomena such as hatred and terrorism.

Elie asked me to assist him with some of the foundation's projects, and of course I agreed. Our dialogues increased—and I developed a particular interest in *The Jews of Silence,* a passionate book in which Elie gave voice to the plight of Soviet Jewry. Then, the following winter, I received an extraordinary invitation to visit the Soviet Union. Elie and I both recognized immediately that this was an unusual opportunity. Quietly, we made a plan.

CHAPTER 29

I T WAS DRIZZLING and cold as I stood with my wife at the edge of a ravine in Kiev, the Ukraine, on a March afternoon in 1987. Across the shallow valley, I could see gentle birches and firs bend and shift gracefully in the moist air, their branches dripping wet snow onto the winding, muddy footpaths below. I had seen hundreds of such scenes before, in places like Idaho and New Hampshire and upstate New York—a familiar landscape of several shades of brown broken by stripes of black and puddles of white, mottled green and gray—signs of the changing season, with its mushy mixture of earth and snow. Yet, however familiar these colors, this was a place I had never been. This was Babi Yar.

It was here, we were told, that the Nazis who occupied this land on September 29, 1941, had ordered the Jews of Kiev to assemble. "Bring a two-day supply of food," the residents were advised—and, of course, "all your valuables."

For several days prior to the actual gathering, our guide explained, the Germans had instigated and encouraged rumors that the Jews would be shipped to Palestine. Thus, instead of the hundreds expected, thousands had come, even perhaps a handful not Jewish at all but other Ukrainians posing as Jews, hopeful that they too might escape, might somehow save their babies from this horrible war. The German soldiers—with the willing assistance of a local militia composed of collaborators, informers and Nazi sympathizers—quickly stole the food from their captives, seized their possessions, then whipped the now-terrified prisoners through a gauntlet and, at its end, ordered the bloodied victims to remove their clothes.

How they must have trembled, I thought, standing where the condemned had stood forty-six years before—neighbors and strangers, humiliated, naked, vulnerable, terror rising in their chests as the killing began. Hidden Nazi machine guns suddenly erupted, sending human beings large and small, ill and infirm, young and old, some dead and some still alive, tumbling into the gully at my feet. Next came the roar of explosive charges, tucked into the walls of the small glen, as they began detonating and raining dirt heavily onto the bodies until, for only a moment, there was silence—soon broken as the carnage resumed. In two days, the Germans executed 33,771 men, women and children on this spot simply because they were Jewish. The Nazi commander received a medal from the Third Reich; no fellow officer, he was told, had killed so many people so quickly.

Although I have been a writer and an editor almost all of my adult life, I can find no words to describe what I felt standing in the mud at Babi Yar. I can say I felt anger and sorrow and hate and love and pity and loss and regret, and that I was vengeful—and all that would be true. But I felt those emotions all at once and, with them, I was empty. I wanted to do something, but there was nothing to do.

Then, alone in my silence, another thought came to me: *Dorfman. Dorfman . . . There probably were Dorfmans at Babi Yar. Or at Auschwitz.*

Or Buchenwald. Had I been born near here, I too would have been a vic-tim—helpless, naked, terrified. For the first time, I am facing the catastro-phe, the Holocaust. These are my people.

And in that moment I knew: *I am no longer the same person as before. Nothing will ever be the same for me. My God, I am a Jew.*

FINALLY, LORETTA BROKE the silence. "What do the Germans say?" she asked the guide.

"Excuse me?"

"Germans visit Babi Yar, don't they?"

"Yes."

"What do the Germans say?" Loretta repeated.

"If they were old enough to be in the war," the guide replied, "they say they served in Africa."

"Of course," Loretta replied, nodding. "What else could they say?"

For a few seconds, we stood quietly in the rain. "Maybe we should leave," our guide finally suggested, "before we're really soaked."

We hurried to a waiting black Volga, the ubiquitous Soviet automo-bile. Loretta and I slipped into the backseat, and the driver threaded the car through the downpour, heading across Kiev to Saint Sophia Cathe-dral. In the silence, I considered how we'd gotten here:

As the editor of *Parade*, I had been invited to tour five cities in the Soviet Union with my wife and to arrange a similar tour in the United States for Vitaly Korotich, editor of the popular Soviet magazine *Ogonyok*, and his wife, Zinaida. Both Vitaly and I had agreed—and this was critical to the exchange—to write our impressions of the other's land for articles to appear simultaneously, side by side, in *Parade* and in *Ogonyok*.

My invitation had come a few weeks earlier in a telephone call from

Oleg Benyukh, the editor of *Soviet Life* magazine, who also was a deputy to the Soviet ambassador to the United States in Washington, D.C.

"Is this possible?" he asked.

"I'll let you know," I said. After speaking with Loretta, I placed a call to Charles Wick, a friend who was then director of the United States Information Agency.

"Is this a good idea, Charlie?" I asked.

"Yes," he told me. "By all means, this is a very good idea. Not only will you be able to decide for yourself whether their new policy of openness—what they call *glasnost*—is real and whether it will continue. But, even more important, you'll have an unprecedented opportunity—and responsibility—to write directly to Soviet citizens in their language. I really think you should do this, Walter. We'll help you in any way we can."

I told Charlie that we'd make the trip.

"Good," he said. "Tell Loretta I guarantee we'll get you out . . ."

He paused.

"Even if it takes ten years."

"Thanks!" I said, laughing. "That's very reassuring."

His humor notwithstanding, Charlie Wick was good to his word. His agency, working with Oleg Benyukh, skillfully arranged all of the necessary visas for our two-week trip, and the United States Information Agency staff also helped me to plan the Korotich tour of Chicago, Knoxville, New Orleans, New York City and Washington, D.C. Loretta and I would see Moscow, Leningrad, Volgograd, Kiev and Tbilisi. Before we left, though, I had one more conversation with Elie Wiesel. We discussed the possibility of me speaking on behalf of oppressed Soviet Jews.

QUESTIONS HAD STARTED to tug at me a few days before our visit to Babi Yar. After about an hour's drive from Moscow, Loretta and I had arrived at Zagorsk—a monastery described as "the center of Russian Christianity" by Vladimir Alexeev, an editor from Novosti, the Soviet press agency, who was our translator throughout the trip. "Tourists often come here," Vladimir added.

I was curious. Here, I knew, was a nation that discouraged religion, that treated notions of God as mere myth, that regarded spiritual icons solely as objects of art, a society where atheism was held to be the ideal. *How could there be believers?* I wondered. *And if there were, how did they learn to believe?*

Zagorsk, I discovered, was a complex of colorful buildings, some of them five centuries old. The oldest structure, built in 1422, was also the smallest—the Troitskaya Cathedral. On its walls were a series of icons, some tracing the Crucifixion of Christ, painted by Andrei Rublev. As we entered this cathedral, also known as the Church of the Trinity, we were joined by a tall young priest named Longin. His beard was lush and long, and his large brown eyes were dark as earth. He wore flowing black robes, his hands concealed in their folds.

A rope split the church into distinct halves. On our side, people queued up single-file to kneel before a priest who stood unobtrusively near a far wall. On the other side was, well, an audience—groups of visitors who had come to see a museum, not a house of worship. I heard the notes of a hymn in the air, a haunting and penetrating melody that I did not recognize. *And where*, I wondered, *is the choir?*

"Longin," I said, "the hymn is wonderful, but I don't see a choir."

"As the people walk through," he explained with a smile, "they take up the hymn, and it stays on their lips until they leave. The believers are the choir. This choir has new members every day. The singing never stops."

The singers, not surprisingly, were mostly older people bundled up against the cold. Yet I also spotted several small children and a boy of about thirteen—and suddenly I was unsettled by the memory of another thirteen-year-old boy in a church not much larger than this one, demanding, "If there's a God, strike me dead!"

My eyes started to fill—not for me but rather for the *moment*: I was moved by the conviction of a continuing hymn, the sound of individuals standing tall against the overwhelming tide of their larger society. And I began to sense, maybe for the first time, what I myself believed.

"Longin," I asked as we were leaving, "how did you come to be a priest?"

"At first, like the other children in my village," he told me, "I was told the stories of the Bible as tall tales. Then—I can't remember precisely when—I started to hear the stories differently. I learned to believe, to have faith."

"But that's not what was intended?" I asked.

"No," he said, "they were told to the children as legends, not to be taken to be true."

"Why you?" I asked.

"Since all the children read the same pages," he replied, "I don't know why I was chosen by God to have faith, only that I'm truly thankful that I do—and that my life is here."

I CONSIDERED Longin's answer again as we rode quietly away from Babi Yar. His words also had come to mind two days before, when we were in Volgograd. We had been told by our guides that only two buildings there had survived World War II, when the city was called Stalingrad. The Nazis had been defeated at Stalingrad after a long and bitter siege in 1942 and 1943. The intensity of the warfare was evidenced by the discovery afterward of more than a thousand shell fragments for each square yard of earth on the plain called Mamayev, where the front-line troops had faced each other—land on which today stands a war memorial.

It was snowing when we wound our way up a long series of steps to that monument—a concrete statue of Motherland, what the Soviet citizens called *Rodina*—rising hundreds of feet in the air. Her body faced what would have been the march of the invading German army, a sword in her right hand raised high, her head turned back to her people, her left arm extended, imploring them to join her, to fight, to die if they must. Her meaning was unspoken but clear: Follow me. The stark contrasts of this enormous country, this nation of eleven time zones, suddenly seemed to blanket me like the falling snow in a confusing flurry of ideas, starting with the memory of Zagorsk and Longin's extraordinary leap of faith. As we stood in silence, I hoped that in time I'd be better able to sort out this blizzard of images that confounded and moved me as we looked up at the tall monument.

Only an hour later, we were in an elevator in an eight-story, cement-block building on Shemenko Street in Red Square. We were about to have lunch with a poet, Tatiana Baturina, in her apartment. Tatiana opened her door and greeted us with a wide smile.

"Welcome!" she said. Then, her English vocabulary exhausted, she immediately looked to our translator, Vladimir Alexeev, for help.

Our knowledge of Russian was no better. "Vladimir," I suggested, "it looks like you're going to get to do a lot of talking."

Tatiana was forty and slender, with the face of a model: soft features, large light-brown eyes, creamy cheeks, and ebony hair styled short. She wore black corduroy Levi's with a pink and maroon feathered blouse, no jewelry and only faint makeup. Her apartment was large—three or four rooms—with polished mahogany units lined with books, some written by her. Persian rugs were scattered about her living room, which also boasted a color television.

After a lunch of fresh vegetables, slices of pork and a chiffon dessert, Tatiana—through Vladimir—started to talk about her work. She'd written seven books of poetry, she said, and had visited Afghanistan, an experience that had so touched her, she had not spoken about it for three months.

"What is it that the poet concerns herself with?" I asked.

Vladimir translated.

"I am dedicated to explore the life of the soul," she replied.

Her response surprised me—not at all what I had expected but, under the circumstances, compelling.

"Are you a Communist?" I asked.

"Yes," she said.

"Are you an atheist?"

"Yes, of course."

"I'm baffled," I said. "If you do not believe in God, how do you conceive a soul? Perhaps we define the concept in a different way. Can you define 'soul' for me?"

Tatiana grew agitated, speaking at length with Vladimir. "It is complicated," she finally replied through him, "and it is not possible to state simply. Can you?"

To my surprise, I nodded.

"What is the soul?" Vladimir asked.

"Our soul is our essence," I replied, and I realized that, with no conscious preparation, I finally had answered for myself a question that had tugged at me since the morning I'd asked, "Is there a God?" Now I understood. I *did* believe—but not in the same way, I knew, as the people who sat with me in that Lutheran church so long ago. I was more like Longin: I heard stories differently.

Vladimir repeated my sentence, and Tatiana became animated. "More," she encouraged. "Please continue."

I nodded.

"Our soul is the very essence of life," I began, "and denying it does not destroy it. Our soul, this spirit within us, is who we really are. It is what binds us together as human beings and what separates us from all other living things."

"Do *you* believe in God?" Vladimir asked.

"Let me answer with a question," I said: "If a single drop of water taken from a raging stream, is the stream forever altered?"

"I don't know," Vladimir replied, before translating for Tatiana.

"I think it is," she said. "What do you think?"

After more than thirty years, I finally felt that I could answer with confidence. "I believe it would be forever altered," I said. "And the stream in which we flow is God. Thus, every life, every soul, has value—and we, unavoidably, are part of each other."

It was as if all the readings and the observations of those three decades, the many dialogues with Elie Wiesel, suddenly came together in a coherent flow: If, as the Bible suggests, we were created in God's image, then it seemed likely to me that the Scriptures meant *our souls*, which could be eternal, *were created in God's image*—not our bodies, which are not everlasting.

WHEN WE RETURNED to Moscow from Kiev, our host, Vitaly Korotich, was eager to hear our impressions. I spoke of the revelation I'd had in Tatiana Baturina's apartment, that *all human beings are God's children*. And I described how, at Babi Yar, I had tried in vain to grasp how one human being could so hurt another—thousands perishing, one by one. I told Vitaly how I'd watched the birches bend so silently in the rain at Babi Yar and had said to myself, "This horrible place of death . . ."

"And of hope," he quickly interjected.

"Hope?" I asked, puzzled.

He nodded.

"I will tell you a story about Babi Yar," he said, "a true story you have not heard before."

At fifty-one, Vitaly Korotich was eight years older than I, and he was a native of Kiev. He spoke English easily, and his eyebrows arched continually above his pink face and bright brown eyes as he talked. I knew that this man of good humor, though modest and unassuming, was a poet and an author of considerable intellect and courage. In the pages of *Ogonyok*, he had published several provocative and critical articles previously banned by the authorities. Stretching the limits of *glasnost*, he had in fact introduced investigative reporting to the Soviet press. Quickly, *Ogonyok* had become the nation's most eagerly sought publication, its 1.5 million copies whisked off newsstands within an hour.

"Yes," I encouraged Vitaly, "please tell me about Babi Yar."

"The Nazis," Vitaly said, "started with the mass murders in those first two days, which you know about. But it did not stop there. The Germans executed more Jews, then Communists, prisoners of war, anyone. By war's end, hundreds of thousands of people had been murdered at Babi Yar, their bodies in piles under the dirt."

He paused.

"And then the Nazis became concerned for themselves. The battle of Stalingrad did not go well for them, and elsewhere their losses were mounting. Faced with the prospect of defeat, the Nazis worried that their horrible crimes would be discovered and that they'd have to account for them. So they tried to destroy the evidence of their terrible deeds. Before the war's end, the German soldiers forced the Jewish prisoners who were still alive to exhume, then burn the bodies of the dead. The stench of so many decomposing corpses was unbearable, and many of the prisoners were able to work only for an hour or so. Kiev, I remember, was in smog, a heavy, thick, stinking smog from the burning of the bodies. It was terrible.

"But in this nightmare there emerged a great lesson," he added, "one I could not document until many years after. You see, some of the victims hoped to the end that they'd be saved—others simply could not grasp what was happening—and, tucked in their undergarments or on their persons, were hidden the keys to their flats, as if they would be able to return. The prisoners who had to burn the bodies searched f̶ those keys and concealed them in their own clothes. Late a̶ they'd quietly try each key to see if any would open the loc̶ racks in which they were imprisoned. One night, one worked. Hundreds fled. Most, of course, were cut down by the guards' machine guns. Fifteen made it, though, and six of them are still alive—five in the Soviet Union and one in Israel. Many years after their escape, I found and interviewed the survivors for a movie I was making at the time."

"And the lesson?" I asked.

"The keys to save us all," Vitaly said, "are in the pockets of the dead."

SEVERAL DAYS LATER, in the Sovietskaya Hotel, where we stayed in Moscow, I had trouble sleeping. *Tomorrow*, I thought, *will be my last full day in the Soviet Union. This tour is over.* Still—and this is what troubled me—I had one more invitation. In the morning, I'd be meeting with some of the leaders of Novosti, the Soviet press agency, and I'd be asked to speak.

What am I going to say?

The harder I tried to think, the more confused I became. I turned, fidgeted in bed, arose, walked into the living room, pulled back the drapes to a large bank of windows and looked into the cold Moscow night. *What am I going to say?*

Images of the last two weeks burst in my mind like bubbles in a boiling kettle. But when I tried to hold one—*this is what I'll talk about!*—instantly it would evaporate, only to be replaced by another image: Longin and the church in Zagorsk, the stark shades of Babi Yar, a hundred war memorials, a family of actors singing a haunting Ukrainian melody in their home in Kiev and Loretta playing with their two-year-old daughter, *Sleeping Beauty* delicately performed by the Kirov Ballet in Leningrad, the majesty of that city's Hermitage museum and its precious art, morning lines in Leningrad to see a visiting exhibit of art by the Wyeth family, afternoon lines in Moscow to buy vodka and longer lines to see Lenin's tomb, a Rublev icon restored by craftsmen at the Repin Institute—and the black swastika that remained on that icon, stamped on its back by some anonymous Nazi half a century ago.

I also recalled four elderly men who offered me a matzoh at a synagogue in Tbilisi in Soviet Georgia, while later, in the same town, I heard anti-Semitic jokes. This contrasted sharply with the inviting hospitality of Vitaly and Zinaida Korotich, the lively yet sensitive discussion about human development I had with some eminent professors from the Soviet Academy of Pedagogical Sciences, and the enthusiasm of a group of scientists toward their distinguished university, the Volgograd Polytechnic Institute, which had risen from the rubble of Stalingrad after World War II.

There also was the tense moment in Moscow when, in front of his subordinates, I interrupted the Soviet minister of education in the midst of a barrage of criticisms he had begun to volunteer about my country.

"Mr. Yagodin," I told him, "we can spend the next half hour with you telling me about Vietnam and Grenada and Nicaragua and with me reminding you about Hungary and Czechoslovakia and Afghanistan. At the conclusion of this discussion, both of us will be more annoyed and less convinced than we are right now. However, if you'd like to continue, I assure you I am fully prepared . . ."

He changed the subject.

I'd rather not have another unpleasant exchange like that one because of my speech to Novosti, I told myself as I gazed out the window of my hotel room. *Nevertheless, if I have to . . .*

What am I going to say?

Finally, a few minutes after four in the morning, the fog started to evaporate. The risk was clear: I could minimize the opportunity, play it safe, challenge no one, shake hands and go home. Or I could try to say what I really felt and risk saying the wrong words and embarrassing myself, my magazine and, unintentionally and by association, my country. *After all*, I thought, *I'm no diplomat. I'm an editor—and a guest. I don't have to say a thing. And if I'm silent, who would ever know? Who cares what I say anyway? If, on the other hand, I don't seize the opportunity to be heard . . .*

I considered again the advice that Elie Wiesel had given me when we discussed the Soviet trip back in New York. He told me to wait until just the right moment: "You'll know when," he assured me. And he was confident that I'd find the right words. "Remember," he counseled, "speak the truth to power."

Yes, I understand. I had found my answer.

"Do you know what you're going to say?" Loretta asked when she arose.

"I think so," I said.

A few hours later, we sat in the spacious mahogany-paneled office of Novosti's first deputy chairman of the board, Sergei Ivanko. He faced me across a long conference table. To his left sat George Fediashin, the vice president and director of news, and at his side was Boris Karlov, the leader of the North American department of Novosti.

Loretta sat to my right, and next to her was our translator, Vladimir. But Sergei Ivanko, I quickly realized, needed no interpreter.

"We hope you enjoyed our country," he said in perfect English, "and I trust that you have received all that you have requested."

"We have," I said, "and thank you."

The room went silent; it was an awkward pause.

"I assume you have some interest in my impressions of your country," I finally volunteered, breaking the silence. Loretta began to take notes.

"Yes," Sergei replied quickly, "we do."

"Then," I said, "let me start. First, though, let me say I'm aware that Charles Wick told you of my government's interest in this trip."

"Yes," Sergei confirmed.

"Then please understand that what I'm about to say is only what I feel. I speak not for my government or for my fellow citizens, but for me. My words are mine alone."

"We understand," Sergei said.

Again, silence.

"No one," I began, "can walk among your people, travel through five cities in two weeks and really know you. Much like the people of my own country, you cannot be known that easily. You are like your toy stacking dolls—a shell within a shell, each layer concealing another more interesting layer, then another. I was welcomed into your homes, schools, theaters, museums, religious places, government agencies—but I am an American, aren't I? I see with the eyes of an American.

"What is it that I see?" I continued. "Two symbols come to mind.

"The first is one of great patriotism, *Rodina*. She is in your earth and in your very souls. I saw her face in the great statue at Volgograd and I saw her in the face of a schoolgirl in Tbilisi. I heard her voice when a Moscow poet spoke, when an actor and an actress in Kiev sang after dinner in their home, when one of your filmmakers in Georgia enthusiastically shared his work with me, and when a nine-year-old boy sought to practice his English with my wife during an intermission of the Kirov Ballet.

"The second symbol I see is one of love, and that would be of a grandparent holding the hand of a grandchild. Nowhere—not on any street in any small village or in any large city—did I see a child unattended. Even your schools for small children are impressive. What hope for the future! Your love of family—the strength of your commitment to each other—is inspiring.

"But there is more.

"War permeates the very air you breathe. Its remnants, its scent, its reminders are everywhere. Twenty million of your citizens died in the last world war. No family was unaffected. Thus, I recognize that no one can come here and talk to you about war. You know war in an intimate way. Yet I too have known war. For most of the people I've spoken with during this tour—if not all—I was the first Vietnam veteran they had ever met. And I'm convinced that these individuals do not want war—

and they do not want it with a passion and in a way that is profoundly
personal. But it is equally clear to me that your leaders have tried to pre-
pare you for war. Even as we speak, your brothers, sons and fathers die
in Afghanistan. Hence, your propaganda, some of which starts right in
this room.

"All arguing aside, you know in your hearts that you have not told
the truth about my country. You may want to respond that America has
propagandized too. And I would have to agree. But should you and I
stop there? You can see that there are no scales on my eyes. I know
there are basic, fundamental differences between our societies, but
maybe each of us can find some wisdom in the old preacher's sermon:
'What binds us together on this earth as human beings is greater than
what separates us.'

"Thus, I'd like to help you to understand Americans—certainly not
all, but at least one: me.

"I am descended from anonymous ancestors who could have been
poor people seeking riches or zealots in a noble cause or rabble-rousers
fleeing some mischief, or worse. Further back than a generation or two,
I really don't know who my people were. I am, like so many of my
countrymen, a mongrel. We too have a statue, in New York harbor, and
she calls to people like me, patchwork ancestry and all. I have a bias—a
deep, unyielding bias—favoring the guiding principles upon which my
own nation was founded. This, I know, does not surprise you.

"Why do I tell you what you already know? Because I want to trust
you, and I assume you want to trust me. Well, if this is true, then you
need to understand Americans a little better—the real us, not the propaganda that has been spread too thick for too long.

"As I said, I speak for me, and there are certain beliefs I have as an
American that I cannot compromise. After remarks I've made in various places during the last few days, I'm quite certain you know it's
important to me that Jews be allowed to leave the Soviet Union. It is
even more important to understand, though, that I would feel the same

if the freedom of passage were denied to Christians, Muslims or, for that matter, atheists.

"Who am I to come to your country and to say such things?

"Again, I have no scales on my eyes. I know that the settlers of my own nation slaughtered Indians, that human slavery was endorsed by the Founders in our original Constitution. I'm aware that during World War II my country imprisoned loyal Americans because their parents happened to be Japanese, and only after that war were black soldiers and white soldiers allowed to sleep in the same barracks. I realize that it wasn't until 1954 that our schools were required to be integrated—a momentous decision that took marches, demonstrations, government troops and years to enforce. Worse, I know that racial prejudice, though no longer the law of the land, continues to trouble—and weaken—my country.

"So, who am I to talk to you about Jews? I am a friend who says: What is wrong is wrong.

"I know that the prejudice here is no less evil than any that exists in my own country—and, like all hatred, it is self-destructive. Indeed, it is the foolish Soviet citizen who finds relief in the knowledge that there may be men and women in America who harbor similar hatreds. As I see it, our goal should not be to see how small we can be or how many people we can hurt. Rather, how many can we *help?* What can we do, together, to improve the lot of human beings on earth? Thus, what I ask, I ask out of love: Have not enough Jews been hurt?

"Must we war over this issue? I pray it does not have to come to that. But I cannot be sure it will not. And I know, as you do, that if we fight, our two nations will leave an earth so scorched that even Babi Yar would pale. The first step for each of us is trust. Your great nation has risen from the crumbled ruins of war in less than half a century; it has clothed, educated, housed its people. Intolerance? Surely, *you* are better than that. *We* are better than that.

"I have told you what I sincerely believe. Now, I thank you for your patience, your courtesy, your hospitality, your candor, your generosity. And your warmth. I hope you feel we've responded in kind. This has been a wonderful visit, and I feel I have made friends. I hope you agree. I wish you could understand how deeply I personally have been affected by this visit. Maybe someday you will.

"In the meantime, for all of us a question remains. Maybe we can at least begin to answer it this morning: Will we wage war, or will we wage peace?

"I am for peace."

Sergei Ivanko reached across the table and clasped my hand. "So am I," he said.

Elie Wiesel had confidently assured me that I would know the right moment and the right words. I had spoken for forty minutes, and I had said precisely what I wanted to say.

CHAPTER 30

THE DRIVER WAS SILENT as I sat in the rear seat of the car, moving north on the FDR Drive in Manhattan. It was June 21, 2000, and I had learned only a few minutes earlier that my brother Bill had died in a hospital in Florida. He had been ill for months, gravely ill for weeks, unconscious for days. I had cautioned family members and friends in the preceding weeks not to call my mother when the end came. *I will be the one to tell her.* Now it was up to me to deliver the news.

As the car threaded through the traffic, I closed my eyes, and memories of Bill came to me. I smiled, recalling the morning he played hooky from high school so that he could take his little brother fishing for the first time at Twin Lakes Reservoir in Eastchester. He was seventeen, I was four. I caught my first bluegill that day with a night crawler. I'm sure the fish was no larger than my hand—but, of course, it was a trophy of elephantine proportions to me. Later, one Saturday, Bill brought me to my first baseball game at Yankee Stadium. I don't think I was older than six. I was enthralled with the bustling crowd, the loud waves of noise and, naturally, the popcorn and the hot dogs. My brother kept insisting, "Watch the game!" Finally, laughing, he gave up. "OK," he said, "watch the people."

I thought about the afternoon he gave me a ride home from school on his motorcycle, a Triumph Thunderbird. I was nine. "What's the matter?" he asked, noticing that I was suddenly nervous as I slipped off the seat behind him. I nodded my head to a man shuffling toward us about twenty yards away on the sidewalk. He had cauliflower ears and a flattened nose. "Did he ever bother you?" my brother asked as he dismounted the motorcycle. "No," I said, "but all the kids stay out of his way. He's a scary guy." My brother called out to the man, and I trembled. "No!" I whispered to Bill. "Let's go." He put his hand on my shoulder. "Just watch," he said.

"Do you know who I am?" Bill asked the man, who nodded *yes*. Bill was twenty-two years old, just five feet seven and about one hundred and fifty pounds. The man, who wore the scars of too many rounds in the ring, was a couple of inches taller than my brother and much broader. But Bill also was a fighter. He had boxed competitively when he was in high school and again in the Navy, where he'd had sixteen fights, resulting in fifteen knockouts and a draw. He had been a welterweight when he was a sailor, and he liked to point out that the draw had been with the national *middleweight* champion—an opponent who was a weight-class heavier. Since he was sixteen years old, Bill had not been defeated in the ring or on the street. Still, he was my brother, and I was afraid for him.

"This is my little brother," Bill continued, "and he's afraid of you. Do you think I'm afraid of you?" The man shook his head. "You're right," Bill agreed, "I'm not. And I'm going to hurt you bad if you ever make my brother afraid. Do you understand me?" The man nodded.

"OK," my brother said, "take off." The man walked away quickly. I was astonished. Bill smiled and then, sensing my surprise, told me, "You don't have to worry about a man who looks like that. Worry about the man who made him look like that."

As the car drew closer to Westchester County, I thought about how Bill had raced motorcycles throughout the Northeast for thirteen years. I couldn't help but chuckle when I remembered the day I went with him to a Pennsylvania racecourse. I was ten years old. He had completed his practice run before the race and handed the motorcycle over to me, telling me to take it straight back to the "butts," the staging area. But I noticed that no one was on the track and decided to try the course myself. I rode onto the track, roared into a corner—and spilled. Dozens of people, led by Bill, ran to my aid. I wasn't injured, but I was embarrassed. The bike's exhaust pipes were scratched, nothing serious. Relieved that I was not hurt, Bill just shook his head. Later, as he examined the bike, I asked him what one particular foot pedal was for. He burst into laughter. "That's the rear brake!" he explained. "That's why you went down. You squeezed the front brake going into the turn. Walter, there are *two* brakes on a motorcycle."

Bill became a firefighter in Mount Vernon while I was in the Marine Corps, and he worked as an emergency medical technician on the rescue unit—saving lives, just as his father had at Engine 2, and receiving numerous awards for bravery. He also rose to leadership positions in the Veterans of Foreign Wars, the American Legion, the Masons and the local United Way. But he never made lieutenant in the fire department, even after nearly three decades—a painful disappointment for him, though he admitted it only to me.

As a young man in his twenties, Bill drank because he wanted to. As he grew older, he drank because he had to—although he'd angrily deny that he was an alcoholic when questioned. His first marriage failed, and then his second marriage. Ultimately, alcohol damaged his body and almost certainly led to his death.

What I wanted to remember, though, as the car got closer to my mother's home, was not the aching pain of seeing someone I loved self-destruct but the better times—seeing my brother as a master of ceremonies at a big fund-raising event, watching him expertly navigate a boat at night on Long Island Sound, hearing him tell stories, stories that grew larger and funnier in time. I'd miss the telephone calls between us, him in Florida and me in New York. I thought about how much Bill enjoyed talking to others about my career and how he would eagerly clip newspaper articles that mentioned me, hand out copies of my books, record my appearances on television—and he'd conclude every conversation: "I'm proud of you, little brother."

And, as I sat silently in that moving car, I knew that my mother had been right all along: It was better that Bill hadn't known our secret.

SHE WAS WAITING FOR ME.

My mother was now living in a two-story house in Westchester with my son and his family. Eric was married by this time, and he and his wife, Claudia, had a son of their own, Jonathan. My mother and her second husband, Gene D'Ambra, had moved here from Queens about four years earlier. But Grandpa Gene had died five months before my brother, at the age of ninety-three.

"Would you like some coffee?" my mother offered before I had a chance to pass through the doorway. "How about lunch? Let me make you a sandwich."

"In a little while, Mom," I said. "I'd like to talk with you first."

I kissed her and then led her to her favorite chair in her living room. I sat on the ottoman facing her, reaching over to squeeze her hand.

"Mom," I said softly, "Billy's gone. He passed away a little while ago."

She nodded.

"You knew?" I asked.

"I figured that's why you called me, why you'd come to see me in the middle of a workday. You'd be the one to tell me."

"He was sick a long time," I said, "and he was in a lot of pain, Mom."

"I know," she said, her eyes filling.

She spoke for about a half hour, haltingly through sobs, recalling some of my brother's adventures and misadventures. Then she became angry: "If he didn't drink so much, if he took care of himself, he'd still be here."

I shifted the topic, asking, "Didn't Billy call you almost every day up until his last few days in the hospital?"

"Yes," she said, her voice soft again. "I think he must have known he was going to die, sick as he was, and he wanted to reminisce with me. We talked about a lot of old stuff."

My mother was eighty-seven years old, a woman who had been widowed twice and who had outlived two of her three children. "Walter," she told me, "there's nothing harder than to bury your own child. It's not natural. It's all wrong. I've had to face it with Carol and now with Billy. . . . Thank God you're here."

She began to sob, and I held her.

A FEW WEEKS LATER, in July, I told my mother that I thought I should finally tell our secret to my children, Eric and Melinda.

"Yes," she agreed. "Now with Billy gone, you *should* tell them. They're both wonderful people, and I think they'll understand."

Loretta, Eric, Melinda and I met for dinner on a warm summer night at Naples, a restaurant in the Met Life Building in Manhattan. It was a convenient location, right over Grand Central Station. I was eager to begin.

"I have something to tell you," I started soon after we were seated, "and it has been a secret for a long time."

Eric and Melinda sat quietly, engrossed, absorbing every word. I spoke for some time, sharing every detail I knew.

Eric was then thirty years old, a human-resources executive, a history buff and a passionate outdoorsman. Melinda was twenty-six, a writer and an editor who loves the arts. Both are sensitive, creative, intelligent, world-wise. It was clear that they were surprised but not taken aback.

Eric spoke first. "Dad," he said, "I'm relieved. I'm happy for you—and I'm happy for us." My son intuitively understood the profound relief I felt in finally sharing the story of my birth with him and his sister.

For Melinda, it was confirmation of a long-held suspicion that I was somehow "different" from her late Aunt Carol and Uncle Billy: "Mom, how many times did I say this?"

Loretta nodded.

We discussed the family name, Dorfman, and concluded that it was German but that the family, being Jewish, most likely had come from Eastern Europe. There was, of course, much I could not answer, because I had never attempted to find my real father or brother Herbert.

"Can I discuss this with Grandma?" Eric asked.

I laughed. "She'll be disappointed if you don't," I said.

THE FOLLOWING FALL, Eric told me he wanted to search for the Dorfmans. "I'd like to try to find them," he said, "but I won't, Dad, if it makes you uncomfortable."

I understood his curiosity, his desire to know. "Eric," I told him, "you're a man, and you don't need my approval. It means a lot to me that you've asked first, that you're concerned about my feelings. But

I'm fine with it, son. Go ahead. You have every right to find out about your family. Good luck—and let me know what you find out."

ABOUT SIX MONTHS AFTER Bill's death, a few days before Christmas 2000, Loretta asked me to help Eric in his search.

"Walter," she said, "he's trying so hard, but he hasn't been able to locate either Albert or Herbert Dorfman. Grandma has told Eric everything she can, and so have you, but he's stuck."

"What do you think I should do?"

"Ask Bernie to help him," suggested Loretta.

Bernard Gavzer, one of the most accomplished investigative reporters in the world, is a courageous journalist whose career has included major assignments with the Associated Press, NBC and *Parade*. He is at once tenacious and sensitive, street-smart and sophisticated. And he is my friend.

About seven years earlier, in 1993, I had asked Bernie to find Barry Williams and his mother—a difficult challenge, because the best information I had was more than thirty years old, and I didn't know Mrs. Williams' first name.

"She was," I told Bernie when he pressed me, "simply *Mrs.* Williams. I never heard anybody ever call her anything else."

"What else don't you know?" he teased.

We both laughed, and then I said, "There's one more thing, Bernie. Barry and his mother are alive and well in my memory. If you turn up something bad or tragic about these people, I don't want to know about it. Just tell me you weren't able to find them, OK?"

"I understand," he said.

Two days later, Bernie called to tell me: "Mrs. Williams lives less than a half-mile from you in Westchester County. Barry lives in Oakland, California, and he has an office in San Francisco. And don't worry, nothing bad or tragic has happened to either of them. Mrs. Williams is just like you described her, and Barry is as smart as you said he was. By the way, her first name is Ilza. But I'm not going to tell you anything more. Call and find out for yourself. Here are their telephone numbers. Good luck, my friend . . . enjoy."

Barry, I soon discovered, had been an honors student and a star athlete at Harvard while I was in the Marine Corps, and he also had earned an MBA and a law degree at Harvard. He was multilingual, had vast experience in international business and counseled several corporations.

Mrs. Williams, who had retired years earlier from the New York City school system, visited my home for dinner with my family the following week. She was, as always, the teacher—energizing the conversation as she asked questions of Eric and Melinda. Eric was a graduate student at Mercy College at the time, and Melinda was an undergraduate at Skidmore. Both were quickly engaged in lively dialogue that reminded me of similar conversations at Mrs. Williams' kitchen table when Barry and I were children.

I was like a boy again, I noticed, basking in the approval of Mrs. Williams. Bernie had reported to her that I had graduated from college—in answer to one of the first questions she'd asked him—which meant that I'd kept the promise I had made to her years earlier, when I quit high school to join the Marines. She told me that she was proud of me, that I was on a path to becoming an educated person ("a voyage that never ends," she pointed out), that Loretta and I had built a strong family and that I was contributing to society, as I was supposed to do. And, she observed with some pride, I was teaching others.

Barry and I spoke frequently on the phone after that, and one day he told me how much our conversations had affected him. "Hearing from you again and talking about my mother," he said, "I realized that my achievements are more about Mom than about me. She encouraged us, never gave up on us and believed in us—so much so that we learned to believe in ourselves. Walter, you and I are two among the many she has guided. You know, she made us believe we could do anything."

"Yes," I agreed, "she surely did."

MY MOTHER, who enjoyed writing brief letters to me, gave me an envelope one afternoon early in January 2001, while we were having coffee in her kitchen.

"How about I read it now?" I asked.

"Sure," she said. I opened the envelope and withdrew a single sheet of paper on which she had written:

> Dear Walter,
>   I lived my last years so happily here with Eric, Claudia and Jonathan. I miss Grandpa and I still grieve for Carol and Billy— but, thank God, I had you. The last years have been great. I traveled all over the world with Gene and we enjoyed it so much together. I want you to continue to make the most of your life, as I know you will.
>
>   Love, Mom

"Are you going someplace?" I asked.

"I'm eighty-eight, Walter, and I know I'm near the end—and that's all right. I want you to know I've had a good life these last few years, and Gene and I always appreciated what you and Loretta and Eric and Claudia and Melinda did for us, and now for me alone. So I just want to say thank you."

"Mom," I said, "first, thank *you*. None of the five of us would be with you right now if you had not given me life. Second, it's not your time yet."

"Oh, honey, neither of us can control . . ."

"No," I insisted, interrupting. "Not yet."

"OK," she said, smiling. "We'll see."

BERNIE GAVZER CALLED me with news a few days later. A couple of weeks had passed since I'd asked him to help in the search for the Dorfmans.

"Walter," he told me, "your real father, Albert Dorfman, was buried on January 31, 1965, in a family plot at King Solomon Cemetery in Clifton, New Jersey. He lived at the time of his death at 442 East 20th Street in Manhattan. He was born in 1904, so he would have been about sixty years old. I don't know how he died, and I still haven't located his son Herbert, your brother, but I'm working on it. I'll be back to you."

"Thank you," I said.

Incredible! Albert Dorfman died in 1965. William Anderson died in 1966. So I couldn't have spoken to my real father after all. I had found out about him a year too late, a year after he died. Should I tell my mother that Albert Dorfman is dead? No. She has had to live through two deaths in the last year. Better to wait. Perhaps Bernie will find Herbert. Mom would like that—and, maybe, so would I.

CHAPTER 31

*T*HAT'S PECULIAR, Herbert Dorfman thought, looking at his answering machine. *I wonder who left a Manhattan telephone number without a message. I don't recognize the number. If it's someone who knows me, he'll call back.* Then, glancing back at the unrecognized number, he decided, *Oh, well, I'm curious.*

He dialed the number, but it just rang. He was about to hang up when the line came alive with a recorded voice identifying itself as Bernie Gavzer.

Bernie Gavzer? In retelling this story, Herb later recalled how he had searched his memory for that name. *Oh, Bernie Gavzer—from Leonia! I haven't spoken to him since my daughter was a little girl and friendly with his son. I wonder why he's calling me after all this time.* Herbert decided to leave no message but made a note to call Gavzer the next day.

✁

BERNIE GAVZER picked up the telephone on the third ring.

"Hi, Bernie," the caller announced pleasantly. "This is Herb Dorfman."

"Oh . . . Herb . . . Dorfman," Bernie responded cautiously, taken aback for the moment by the caller's familiar tone.

Herb noticed quickly that Bernie did not seem to recognize him. *Strange,* he thought. *Bernie's not very friendly, considering that I'm returning his call. He sounds surprised. I'll try one more time:* "Herbert Dorfman, Bernie—from Leonia."

Bernie hesitated.

"You don't remember," Herb pressed, "do you?"

Bernie was scrambling, stretching to recall. "Oh, yeah," he replied, "a little bit."

"Well," Herb asked, sensing correctly that Bernie had not contacted him to discuss shared experiences years earlier in Leonia, New Jersey, "why are *you* calling *me* after all this time?"

"Herb," Bernie replied, "I'm doing research for a magazine assignment on some of the people who worked in defense plants during World War II. One of the names I've come up with is an *Albert* Dorfman."

"Well," Herb replied, "my father's name was Albert Dorfman, and I know that he worked in Manhattan during the war at a place that made optical bombsights."

"I'd like to discuss this more," Bernie suggested.

TWO DAYS AFTER Bernie Gavzer reported to me that he had located my real father's grave, he called again.

"I found your brother," he told me.

The words sailed into me: *I found your brother.*

I squeezed the telephone tightly, rapt.

"What did you find out?" I asked.

"Well," Bernie said, "I have to tell you that some of this is amazing. It turns out that I knew him many years ago, when we both were raising families in New Jersey, but I had forgotten all about it. He had no idea, of course, that he was only one of several Herbert Dorfmans I was investigating to track down the son of Albert Dorfman. He was as friendly as could be—all because he thought I was calling him about Leonia. What a coincidence! My son, Adam, is a friend of his daughter, Robin. I've only spoken with Herb over the telephone so far. He's going to be traveling—I think to London—for ten days, so it may be some time before I actually sit down with him. He's seventy-two years old, still very active, and he has the one child, Robin, who's thirty-eight. He and his wife, Esther, also had a son, Andrew, who died when he was only five. Robin works for Disney out in California, but I'm not sure what she does. Herb still has a house with his wife in Leonia and an apartment in the East Sixties in Manhattan."

"What's he like?" I asked.

"I'll be able to answer that better after we meet in person. It has been a long time since I last saw him, Walter, but I do know a little about his background. What I can tell you is that Herbert Dorfman worked his way through college, began as a print reporter but distinguished himself later as a producer of television news shows and documentaries. He's a very capable guy."

"He's in our field?" I asked, the astonishment apparent in my voice.

"I know," Bernie said, "the coincidence struck me too."

I SAT BACK IN MY CHAIR. If Bernie was right, this is the same Herbert Dorfman whose name used to roll in the credits after the evening news. More than once, my mother had whispered, "That could be your brother, Walter." I decided to wait, though, before I told her. I wanted to be sure.

CHAPTER 32

W ALTER," BERNIE TOLD ME, "I'm going to have lunch next week with Herbert Dorfman. How far do you want me to go?"

"Use your judgment," I said. "You have a lifetime of experience, pal. I trust you completely. If you sense for any reason that it would be better that he doesn't know about me, or if you think he's too frail to hear the truth, continue the cover story, say goodbye, and we'll just let it go. The last thing I want is to upset this man's life or hurt him."

"All right," Bernie said, "I'll take care of it. I'll call you right after the lunch. Where can I reach you?"

"Loretta and I will be in Key West on vacation. Leave a message with my assistant, AnneMarie, at the office. Believe me, I'll be calling in after lunch."

"I'm sure you will," Bernie replied. "Does your mother know yet that I found Herb?"

"Not yet," I said. "I'm going to wait. And Bernie . . . thank you."

ANNEMARIE PALMER, in typically efficient style, quickly brought me up-to-date on the business of the day and got the answers she needed, then listed my phone messages, concluding, "And Bernie Gavzer left a number for you. Do you want me to get him for you?"

"Would you, please?" I asked, clasping the cell phone to my ear. I stood alone in the warm sand outside the Sunset Key house that Loretta and I were renting with two of our friends, John and Marilyn Rosica. It was in the middle of the day in the middle of the last week of February 2001.

"He's on the line," AnneMarie announced before disconnecting herself from the call.

"He knows," Bernie began.

BERNIE HAD INVITED Herbert Dorfman to lunch at the Arte Café on West 73rd Street in Manhattan—and his guest was late.

Herb apologized when he arrived, explaining that he'd had difficulty finding a place to park his car.

Astonishing! Bernie reflected. *What kind of guy uses a car on a weekday to drive from the East Sixties to the West Seventies?*

The two men began to discuss news projects and stories told in print and broadcast—the sort of conversation most journalists find endlessly interesting. Bernie observed Herb carefully throughout and, finally, made his decision:

"Herb," he said, "can we talk some more about your father?"

"Sure."

"Did your father live in Stuyvesant Town in Manhattan when he died?"

"Yes, he did."

"And he worked at Farrand Optical, the defense plant I mentioned, during the war?"

"Yes," Herb said, adding, "in fact, I can remember how he described the ingenuity of the devices made at that factory to my Uncle Dick. My father was really impressed with the genius of their simplicity, how they worked so well."

Bernie reached into his jacket, withdrew a sheet of paper and handed it to Herb.

"How did you get this information?" Herb asked, puzzled as he read the cemetery information about his father's burial, accurate to the last detail, even to the number and location of the Dorfman family plot. Later, Herb told me how he'd sat there, saying to himself: "The real question is not how he got this information but *why*. Why would Bernie Gavzer go to all this trouble?"

But before Herb could ask his second and more important question, Bernie responded quickly to the first: "It really doesn't matter how I got the information, Herb. I've been a reporter for a long time, and you know there are many ways to find these things."

"*Why* did you seek out this information?" Herb asked.

Bernie did not hesitate. "Because," he replied as gently as possible, "you have a brother."

Herb, who had been raised as an only child and knew of no siblings, was silent for a few seconds. When he did start to speak again, it was to resurrect their earlier conversation about television projects. It was as if he had not heard Bernie's startling news. Bernie decided to go along for the moment, sitting quietly and nodding until his words had registered.

Herb rambled on and then suddenly stopped. "Let's go back," he told Bernie. "What are you saying?"

"You have a brother," Bernie repeated, then he started to describe me in broad strokes—primarily as a recognizable person in communications—but he withheld my name and specific details.

Herb changed the subject again and then, a few minutes later, asked another question about Bernie's search.

After Bernie answered that question, Herb started to discuss a television project, then interrupted himself again and asked: *"Who* is my brother?"

"His name is Walter Anderson," Bernie began, "and for the last year he has been the chief executive officer of *Parade* magazine. Before that, he was the magazine's editor for twenty years. It's possible you might recognize him as an author—he's written a number of books. He also created a one-man play called *Talkin' Stuff* and performed it at Ford's Theatre in Washington. And he's been interviewed on radio and television many times. He's done a lot of other things too. There's a lot of information freely available about him. It would be easy for you to check him out. You also might want to know that he has been married to the same woman for more than thirty years, and they have two children and a grandson. He's also my friend."

Herb held up his hand and started to rise. "I have to fill the meter," he told Bernie, then excused himself and left the table.

Herb would later admit that he rarely had felt such deep resentment. "Who is Bernie Gavzer to ask me these questions and to tell me things like this that can change my life?" he muttered to himself as he walked to his car. "What am I, a Communist spy or something?"

Oblivious to the people walking past, Herb stared absently at the parking meter. *I don't know what to make of this,* he told himself. *Maybe I should just get in my car and drive home, and then this will all go away.*

He hesitated.

Bernie's not a bad guy, Herb thought upon reflection. *The thing is, this is hard information to deliver, and he obviously thinks I can handle it. Can I? I don't know. I'm not sure what I feel right now. Well, in any case, it wouldn't be nice for me to leave Bernie sitting there. This can't be easy for him either. I'll go back and see where this goes.*

He dropped two quarters into the meter.

After Herb returned to the table, the two men deliberately ignored the sibling issue. Instead, they talked about television coverage. As they were leaving, Bernie invited Herb to a poker game.

"I'll let you know," Herb promised.

ALONE IN HIS APARTMENT, Herb sat quietly, too stunned to call his wife or daughter. Hours rolled by. He did not move, his mind replaying again and again the conversation he'd had with Bernie. He knew that something big had just happened and his life would not be the same again. So many questions. Should he take the first step and reach out? Should he ignore it? What does it all mean?

He was startled by the ring of his telephone.

"Hello," Herb said.

"Hello," I replied. "This is Walter Anderson."

CHAPTER 33

I COULD HEAR the uncertainty in his voice.

"This is . . . a surprise," Herb began. "You can expect . . . well, I have a lot of questions."

"Not the least of which," I interrupted, "is whether or not this is true."

"Yes, of course," he replied.

"Herb," I said softly, "more than anyone, I think I know how you must feel. I've been living with this secret for decades. You've been living with it for a couple of hours. I can still remember what I felt when I was first told."

I spoke for several minutes. I repeated some of the details Bernie Gavzer had already told him about me and my family, and I gave him some of the historical information that my mother had shared with me.

"This is simply amazing," he said.

I assured him that I was genuinely pleased to find him, but I said I had no expectation: "I recognize, as you do, that nothing may come of this, that the gulf of our separate lives may be too wide for us to bridge."

"True enough," he said.

"If, however," I continued, "you'd like to find out more—either to satisfy your curiosity or to determine whether this is true or an unfortunate error—well, Herb, I'd be happy to meet with you in person. In fact, I'd look forward to it."

He paused and then said, "OK, we'll meet. That's a first step. But you have to realize, I have a lot of questions. This is new to me, and it's something I never expected. So I should be skeptical."

"I understand," I said. "But if my mother is correct, your biggest question will be answered when you see my face."

"What do you mean?" he asked.

"My mother says I have my father's face, only with a different eye color and thinner lips. Since I've never seen a picture of the man, you'll know the truth a millisecond before I will, because you know what your father looked like."

"When would you like to get together?" he asked.

"As soon as possible," I replied, and we arranged to meet in his apartment the following Wednesday evening at seven o'clock.

LORETTA HAD PATIENTLY WAITED while I was on the cell phone but now was eager to hear every detail of the conversation. "How did it go?" she asked as soon as I stepped into the kitchen of the vacation house.

"Pretty well, under the circumstances," I said. "He sounded tentative, naturally, and he's obviously still surprised. Bernie's judgment was right, though. He can handle it. He's solid."

"Did you like him?"

"I think so," I replied. "He sounds like a really nice guy. I'll know better next week, though. I'm going to visit him in his apartment."

"You are? That *is* quick."

"I've been waiting thirty-five years, Loretta, and now I'm finally going to meet Herbert Dorfman, like him or not—and I'll find out more about my real father. Herb even promised to have a picture to show me."

"How do *you* feel?"

"Excited. Nervous. Anxious. To tell you the truth," I said, "I'm not sure how I feel, but I'm really glad it's gotten this far."

"Are you going to tell your mother now?" asked Loretta.

"You bet I am," I answered. "I'll talk to her as soon as we get back to New York."

"How do you think she'll take the news?"

"*My* mother?"

We both started to laugh.

HERB PLACED THE TELEPHONE onto its receiver and settled back into his chair. He sat quietly for another hour, mulling our conversation, then reached for the telephone and called his daughter in California.

"Robin," he asked, "are you sitting down?"

"Yes," she said. "Why?"

"I have some news."

"Is it bad news?" she asked. "Did someone die?"

"No."

"What is it?"

"I have a brother," Herb said.

"What did you say?"

"I have a *brother*."

"I can't believe it," Robin responded, her voice even.

"Well, I don't think he would have gotten on the phone and spoken with me if it wasn't true."

"You *spoke* with him?"

"Yes, I did," Herb replied. Then he described in detail the conversations he'd had with Bernie Gavzer and the man claiming to be his brother.

"Bernie *Gavzer*? Adam's father? From *Leonia*?"

"Yes," Herb confirmed, "an incredible coincidence! That's the reason I called Bernie back in the first place."

"This is surreal," Robin said. "Tell me more about Walter Anderson."

"He's done a lot, Robin. I'm sure there's a good deal of information about him on the Web."

"Wait," Robin said. "I'll call you back."

THE TELEPHONE RANG.

"He *is* your brother!" Robin announced. "I found plenty about him quickly—pictures too—on the Web. I can tell you that he looks a little like you in photos from when you were younger, but he looks even more like the photos of your father. Actually, he has an *amazing* resemblance to your father. You'll see when you meet him in person."

"You know," Herb said, "Walter told me that, if his mother is right, my biggest question will be answered when I see his face."

"When are you going to meet him?" asked Robin.

"Wednesday night . . . in my apartment."

"Call me immediately after."

Herb looked at his watch and decided that Esther should be at their home in Leonia by now. He dialed the number, and his wife answered on the third ring.

"Hello," she said.

"Esther," Herb responded, "do I have news for you!"

CHAPTER 34

M Y MOTHER'S EYES WIDENED. "No kidding!" she exclaimed. "So he *was* the Herbert Dorfman whose name appeared on television."

"It sure seems so, Mom."

She hesitated and then spoke softly. "Al is gone, isn't he?" she asked, her eyebrows rising.

"Yes, Mom, he died in 1965."

She sighed and was briefly silent. "So, Walter, you couldn't have found your real father anyway."

"No, Mom," I said, "he died a year before you told me."

She sat quietly for a few seconds more and then said, "Well, Al had ulcers awfully bad. The last time I saw him was in 1954, when you were ten, and he wasn't feeling well even then. Al didn't complain—but I could see he wasn't right."

Again she became quiet.

I interrupted her reverie: "Is that when you broke it off?"

"Yes," she said, "but the truth is, we never had relations after you were born. I was too scared. We saw each other several times over the years, but only to talk. I made Al agree not to see me again. I told him it was just too dangerous. I was more terrified than ever that Willie would find out the truth about you. You see, as you grew older, you began to look even more like Al."

I nodded.

"And, *finally*, Al agreed. But I have to tell you, it was difficult. After we said goodbye, I watched him walk away. It was all I could do not to scream, 'Come back!' It hurt for a long time—but it was the right thing to do."

"You really loved him, didn't you?"

"I sure did. I have to say I thought about trying to find Al myself after I told you the truth—but I knew Al had married again. However much I wanted him back, I wouldn't do something like that and hurt his new family. And, as you know better than anyone else, I didn't want Billy or Carol to find out. So I did nothing."

"Not exactly, Mom. You fell in love with Grandpa Gene."

"That's true—and I would never have met or married Gene if I had taken up with Al again. Do you remember how Gene and I met?"

"Yes," I said, chuckling. "You met through a computer dating service, and you were *last* on his list! You told me that he almost didn't call you."

"It's funny how things work out, isn't it?" she said, smiling. "I'm so glad I married Gene. We had a good thirty years."

"Now I guess this news about Herb makes you pretty unhappy?" I teased.

She laughed loudly. "I'm thrilled!" she declared. "All these years I wanted you to meet your brother . . ."

She stopped suddenly, and her eyes filled.

"Mom?" I asked.

"It's OK, honey. You know, sometimes I cry when I'm happy." She paused to dry her eyes. "And now tell me everything about Herb. Everything!"

I slowly recounted my conversations with Bernie and Herb, studying my mother's face as I spoke. *She's still beautiful*, I thought. *And when she smiles that certain way . . . dimples.*

When I had finished filling her in, I asked, "Mom, do you have any regrets?"

"At eighty-eight?" she exclaimed, smiling wide. Then she hesitated, mulling her thoughts, and the smile faded.

"I've had pain, Walter. I'll never get over losing Carol and Billy, but I think I've had a good life. Hey, I know I'm glad I had you. Of that I'm sure. Maybe I would have done some other things differently. Regrets, though? No, I honestly don't think so. But . . ."

"But?" I interrupted.

"It was very important to Al that his two sons meet. That was *his* regret. So I'm very happy that you are going to see Herb."

THE ELEVATOR climbed to Herbert Dorfman's floor, high in a building about a half block from the FDR Drive and the East River. My stomach fluttered.

Thirty-five years had passed since I first heard my mother say this man's name. Now we'd be meeting face to face. *What is he like?* I wondered. *What was my father like? Wait! Is this a mistake?*

Before I could change my mind, the elevator doors opened.

CHAPTER 35

Herbert Dorfman was waiting for me in the hallway.

"Walter?" he asked, smiling.

"Yes, Herb, that's me," I replied, smiling back.

"Well," he added warmly, "come on in."

I followed Herb into his one-bedroom apartment, its walls and bookshelves filled to brimming. He looked older than I, as I had expected, and he wore glasses and had a mustache. Impatiently, I tried to see beyond those features, looking for a link. I remembered my mother's caution: "I'd guess that each of you resembles your father more than you do each other. But from what Al told me, you look more like him than Herb does. I'm sure Herb will notice that right away."

Don't stare, I reminded myself. *Don't make this any more awkward than it already is.*

He was about my height, and I noticed that, curiously, he didn't have brown eyes like our father but hazel eyes like mine—and both were focused solidly on me.

After shaking hands, Herb led me to a small couch. He sat across from me, and for several minutes we made small talk, retracing our conversation from the week before. Then Herb suddenly interrupted himself mid-sentence:

"You *do*!" he exclaimed.

"Excuse me?"

"Walter, you really *do* look like my—*our*—father. It's quite amazing, I have to say." Herb then reached for a manila file folder and said, "Here are some pictures. You can see for yourself."

Rarely have I wanted to do anything as much as I wanted to open that folder, but I inexplicably hesitated.

What's wrong with me? I've been waiting thirty-five years to see the face of this man. What's holding me back? Pick it up. Take a look.

My skin tingled. My stomach was uneasy. *Oh, go ahead. Pick it up.*

I reached toward the folder, which Herb had placed on the coffee table, and lifted it to my lap. I opened it slowly and glanced at the first picture. It was a black-and-white photograph of a man probably in his late twenties, with a small, almost shy smile. I recognized the hairline, the eyes, nose and cheeks.

Mom was right.

HERB WAS THOUGHTFUL and polite, fully composed. He spoke slowly, seeming to weigh the impact of each word. "I guess we don't know where this will all lead," he said. "Or maybe, Walter, it will lead nowhere at all. Naturally, I have a lot of questions, as I know you do too. And I'll answer any questions I can for you. But I was curious—I think you'll understand. Why did you wait so long to contact me?"

"I gave my word to my mother that I would not search for you or our father. It was important to her."

"Why did you contact me now?"

"My sister, Carol, died many years ago of breast cancer. She was a young woman at the time. My brother Bill died last year. He was sixty-eight. My mother did not want them to know her secret. After Bill died, my mother released me from my promise."

"Does she know that you found me?"

"Yes."

"How does she feel about that?"

"Herb," I replied, "my mother's ecstatic. I'm sure she's dying to meet you in person. I think you'll find—*if* you meet her—that she knows more about you . . . well, let's just say more about you than you might expect."

"I don't understand."

"Herb, your father was very proud of you, and he talked with my mother about you until you were in your twenties, when they stopped seeing each other."

He raised his eyebrows. "This is a little disconcerting, Walter. I'm sure you can understand."

"Of course," I assured him. "It's a little like finding out that someone has been watching you without your knowledge."

I then reached into my briefcase and withdrew two pictures of my mother—one taken about the time she would have been seeing Albert Dorfman and one taken more recently—and handed both to Herb.

"Oh, my God!" he exclaimed, his composure broken for the first time. "This is incredible! Walter, your mother looked a lot—I mean a *lot*—like my own mother when she was young."

Herb left the room but returned quickly with a decades-old black-and-white photograph of a smiling woman who did, in fact, resemble my mother when she was younger. "Our father certainly knew what he liked!" I observed, and we both began to laugh.

TWO HOURS LATER, as I walked south on York Avenue to my own apartment, my mind replayed the images of the evening. Then, suddenly, I became enraged as the memory of all my beatings as a child pushed aside those newer images. *Who was he to beat me? He wasn't even my real father.*

It lasted only seconds—maybe even less than a second. But, however long, it was a blinding rage that I had not known since the day I returned from Vietnam and confronted the man who had raised me in Mount Vernon so many years ago. And then, as quickly as the anger had come, it was gone.

What difference does it make now? I realized.

LORETTA ANSWERED the telephone on the first ring. "Tell me everything," she said.

"Herb *is* a nice guy," I began, "I think if he wasn't my brother, he'd be my close friend. It's just incredible how much Herb and I have in common—but even more amazing is the fact that we had not met before. Herb and I have worked with or around so many of the same people."

I proceeded to tell my wife about our mutual acquaintances, including Jack Anderson and Julia Child. At the same time that Jack was *Parade*'s Washington bureau chief and Julia was our food editor, both were also contributors to *Good Morning America*, where Herb was then the head writer. "And do you remember when I considered giving up print journalism to go on television with NBC—before I joined *Parade*?" I asked Loretta. "Well, Herb was then a writer and a producer for the *Today* show on NBC. Could you imagine? It goes on and on. We have so many related interests and abilities. It's a little like parallel lives."

"What about your father?" asked Loretta.

"Herb told me our father was one of six children—five boys and a girl—born near the turn of the century in Russia, in Odessa. One of Al's younger brothers may have been born in the United States. The family emigrated here before 1910 through Ellis Island, so it's possible that Dorfman could have been a name assigned to the family by a clerk at Ellis Island. It's not a Russian name. Anyway, all of Albert's siblings are dead."

"Did you ask Herb why his father died so young, in his sixties?"

"I did. Herb says the doctors called his condition rheumatoid arthritis, but he says they told him it was really some sort of collagen disease."

"You have to get checked for that yourself now," said Loretta.

"I will," I agreed. "But let me tell you what else I found out. Albert grew up in the heavily Jewish section of East New York. Herb said that although our father later became quite well-read on his own, he didn't finish high school and was hurt by his lack of formal education. Herb said he held a lot of jobs. He ran a photography booth at the 1939 World's Fair and later ran a garment business. He was in the Army for two years but was discharged early in the war because he had ulcers. I remember Mom talking about his ulcers too."

"Walter, you sound so excited about all this," said Loretta. "How do you feel now?"

"Good," I said. "I'm glad Eric made this happen. There's something I don't understand, though. On the one hand, it's as if I've known Herb a long time. Talking to him is a little like talking to myself. But, on the other hand, I think I'm missing something. It will come to me. Anyway, Herb and I definitely are going to spend more time together."

"When are you going to talk to your mother again? She's going to be really excited."

"I'm going to see her tomorrow—and I have a surprise for her."

"What's that?"

"A picture of Albert Dorfman."

"THAT'S AL!" my mother exclaimed, giddy as a toddler, grasping the picture tightly with both hands. "Can I keep this picture?"

"Would you give it back to me if I asked?" I teased.

She kissed me on the cheek and hurried into her den, where she opened an old oak hope chest, rummaging inside until she found a suitable frame. She replaced its photograph with the one I had given to her. She then returned to the living room and, smiling broadly, slowly— almost ceremoniously—placed the picture of Albert Dorfman next to one of me.

"What do you think?" she asked.

"Mom," I replied, "what do *you* think?"

"I'm so happy," she said. "Thank you for this. And there's something else."

She hesitated, clearly mulling the thought before making her decision.

"Mom," I asked, "what is it?"

"Walter," she said, "*I'd* like to meet Herbert."

CHAPTER 36

M Y MOTHER'S HANDS were more knotted than ever with arthritis, so I knew she had struggled to write the letter to me dated March 11, 2001:

> *Dear Walter,*
>
> *I feel my life is finally complete now that you have found your brother Herbert. Your father would have been pleased. I loved your father, and I know he loved me. We were soul mates . . . I loved Grandpa Gene in a different way. I'm sorry that you never saw your dad. You were too little to remember. He missed watching you grow up, but I know your father often thought of you. Keep well, you two brothers.*
>
> *Love, Mom*

I phoned my mother after reading the letter and promised that some-day I would share it with Herb. "That would be wonderful," she replied. "I'm so happy for you and Herb. The only one who could be happier is Al—and I want to believe that somehow, wherever he is, he knows."

"I understand, Mom. The thing is, are *you* ready to meet Herb?"

"Ready? You bet I'm ready!"

"Ethel," I kidded, "you have to learn to be more enthusiastic."

"When, honey? *When?*"

"April tenth," I replied. "Herb, his wife, Esther, their daughter, Robin, and their grandson, Andrew, are coming to our house for din-ner with Loretta and me. Melinda, Eric, Claudia and Jonathan are coming too. Only Robin's husband, Jeff, will be missing. He has busi-ness that will keep him in California. Now, if *you* don't have other plans . . ."

"*Plans?*" she interrupted, laughing. "*What* plans? I can't wait."

ROBIN WAS FIRST through the doorway, bustling and laughing. "Hi, *Uncle* Walter!" she exclaimed as she hugged me enthusiastically with one arm while Andrew, her two-year-old son, clung tightly to the other. Herb and Esther—both smiling broadly now, clearly delighted by their daughter's greeting—followed her into our home.

Robin's uninhibited entrance and genuine warmth started the night in the best possible way, but it still took a few hours before the rest of us were at ease. At first, all of the adults—me included—looked like we were playing musical chairs. Each of us seemed compelled to shift seats, reintroduce ourselves and start fresh conversations. Jonathan and Andrew, two little boys only months apart in age, had no such inhibi-tions: They quickly occupied themselves with Jonathan's toys. And, of course, both boys were soon the center of attention.

Dinner, however, was the threshold.

Eric said grace, giving thanks that "our family is together, finally, and complete."

And then Herb made it happen. He glanced toward Robin and said he'd like to tell us how her son got his name. Robin nodded.

Robin, Herb explained, had a brother, Andrew, who died of a brain tumor when he was five and she was almost seven. For all the years that followed, Herb said, the hurt for him and Esther had not healed, and they spoke of the tragedy only rarely.

When Robin gave birth to a boy, she and Jeff decided to surprise her parents by naming him Andrew. Esther and Herb discovered the surprise when they visited the hospital, and they were profoundly moved. A few days later, Herb told Robin how meaningful her quiet gesture had been for him and Esther, finally providing closure to their son's tragic death, and he thanked her.

By the meal's end, Eric's grace seemed to have come true: We were speaking easily, naturally, with each other.

After dinner, Andrew surprised his grandparents and his mother by plopping down in Melinda's lap and *staying*.

"That's amazing," Herb said. "Andrew usually won't sit with anyone but his mother."

A few minutes later, my mother squeezed Herb's forearm lightly, encouraging him to join her on the couch. I studied my mother's face as they spoke. Her joy was palpable, animated and fresh. I noticed that Herb was unmistakably engaged as well, and I sensed that a bond between the two had been cemented. Later, Herb would describe to me how well he and my mother had connected and how much he'd learned from her about his father—things he'd never learned from his own mother, Betty, who had died in 1986.

"HOW DO YOU THINK it went tonight?" Loretta asked me after everyone had gone and we were alone.

"It could not have gone better," I replied. "I wanted two things to happen: First, for Mom to meet Herb—and it's clear they hit it off. I'm sure they'll be on the phone with each other a lot. And, second, I hoped we'd all be comfortable."

"I think we are, Walter."

"Me too."

CHAPTER 37

A L WAS A QUIET MAN," my mother told me as we sat in her
kitchen a few days later, "and he liked to read. He learned a
lot from reading—things that would surprise people."

"Herb told me the same thing," I said. "He described one time when
he was a television producer working on a financial report, and he mentioned to his father that England was temporarily devaluing the pound.
Al then surprised Herb by explaining economic theory and why the
action was necessary. He even predicted what its impact would be, and
Herb said it turned out Al was right!"

"Honey," my mother said, nodding, "*that* was Al. He was so much
smarter than you'd have known from his education. And it came out in
different ways."

"Like what?" I asked.

"Walter, when I first met Al, he made some money on the side by playing cards and shooting pool. I asked him once about it. He told me he was able to win more than he lost because he understood odds, and he made it his business to know more about the people he played against than they knew about him. He wasn't bragging, though. He just said it matter-of-factly.

"And," she continued, "when you were a little boy and started playing pool yourself on Third Street, you reminded me of Al. Do you remember?"

Do I remember? How could I forget?

IT WAS 1956, and I was just twelve but already a pretty good player, mostly from practicing on the table at the Boys Club. I wanted desperately to get in that poolroom on Third Street, just a couple of blocks from our tenement. The best black players from the region went there, and I wanted to watch them—and learn. You had to be sixteen, but I managed to get in one Saturday afternoon with a friend, Jimmy, whose dad was a regular patron. This patient man took me under his wing, and I began playing with him whenever he was there.

Then one day I wandered in when Jimmy's father wasn't there. I was sure I'd be thrown out. Minutes passed. Then I understood: *I belonged!* For the next two years, I'd hurry over there every day after I finished my newspaper route and my homework. Nights, weekends, I also practiced—a quarter a rack—spending the few dollars I was earning each week delivering newspapers.

Of the memories of my childhood, none are more vivid than the smell of cigarettes and beer in that poolroom, the satiny feel of the green felt, the dusty blue chalk. And the sounds—Chuck Berry, Fats Domino, Ray Charles, Little Richard—all heard behind the crack of the balls, the laughter and sometimes the silence. The silence meant something unusual was about to happen: an especially difficult "big-money shot" with big bets riding on it or, occasionally, an argument. Players roared when someone retold a raunchy joke by Moms Mabley or Slappy White or Redd Foxx.

Of the hundreds of men who saw me nearly every day in that poolroom, few knew my name. They called me "you" or "boy" or "kid" until one Saturday when I was fourteen. That's when I earned a new nickname.

I was playing "Fifty" with an older man when I beat him, sinking nineteen balls in a row, the most ever for me. "Keep going!" someone shouted, and all the other games stopped. I could feel the players circling, standing quietly and watching. I continued shooting, making one shot and then the next.

Finally, at thirty, I was faced with a difficult long table shot. Several of the spectators placed bets. I noticed that Jimmy's father, whom I respected immensely, was quiet. "Heart," he once told me, "counts more than skill most of the time. Instead of concentrating on the stakes, try to remember how you've made the same shot before." I noticed that Jimmy's dad didn't bet on my shot, but he did smile.

I leaned over the table to study the angle. *I can do this*, I thought. I pictured it in my mind. More bets. My pulse raced. *Think about the shot.*

I drew back the cue. I made that shot—and the next. Then I missed.

A run of thirty-one! Although I never approached thirty-one again, the feat earned me a nickname:

"Boy," someone called me.

"That's no 'boy,'" Jimmy's dad told him. "That's 'Run.'"

For nearly a month I was hailed, "Hey, *Run,* want to shoot a game?" One time a new player, misunderstanding the nickname, called me Runt. *"Run,"* I corrected—and several players chuckled.

Then, one Saturday afternoon, as I was about to take a shot, I heard my real name shouted—"Walter!"—and my skin tingled.

I couldn't breathe.

Standing in the open doorway was my father, his face red, the veins of his neck working, his hands balled into fists. Several of the players knew my father, who did not play pool, who *hated* pool-rooms, and whose drinking and violent temper stood out even in our neighborhood. It was no surprise, then, that even the folks he drank with had chosen not to tell him that his son was hanging out in a poolroom only a few blocks away. My mother also had warned me to stay out of trouble, understanding what I'd face if my father found out where I was.

No one moved.

"Get home *now*!" he bellowed.

I reached into my pocket, nervously grabbed two quarters to pay for the game and dropped them on the table.

"Move!" he shouted.

I walked briskly to the door of the poolroom. I tried to slide past him, but he cuffed me on the back of the head—a slap that sent me sprawling to the pavement outside.

"If I ever find my son in here again," he threatened, his words slow, his voice low and deep through clenched teeth, "I will close this place."

Still, no one moved.

"*Ever!*" he added.

He beat me on the way home, in the apartment that afternoon and again later that night.

"You will *never* go in there again!" my father shouted.

I didn't. Nor did I ever play pool seriously again.

"MOM," I SAID, "I haven't played a game of pool since I was fourteen, but I would have liked to have played pool with *him*."

"I know Al would have enjoyed that too," she said.

"Sure," I said, laughing now myself. "He would have enjoyed *winning*!"

"I don't know," she replied. "I remember that all of your friends said you were very good."

"Mom, I came to know some players like Albert Dorfman when I was a kid. I'm sure he would have beaten me when I was a fourteen-year-old boy. It would have been fun anyway, but I wouldn't have laid down a bet!"

She laughed.

"Mom," I asked, "what else did you and Al talk about?"

"Oh, everything," she replied. "Al read the newspapers, and he loved to talk about what was going on in the world—and I loved to listen to him. Let's see. Well, he talked a lot about Herbert. He was very proud of Herbert. Herbert was a really good student—like you, Walter. Anyway, Al and Herbert's mother already had been separated many years when we first met, and I know that Herbert lived mainly with his mother. Al had some guilt about that. Funny, though, as I look back, if someone would have heard us talking, they would have thought we had *two* sons. It was 'Herbert *this* and Walter *that*.' I know this sounds a little crazy." She stopped speaking.

"No, Mom, I think I understand. Go ahead."

"OK," she continued. "It was like we were alone on an island when we were together. Does this make any sense?"

"I think it does," I told her. "Did he worry about anything?"

"Being found out by my husband, I'm sure. After all, I reminded him constantly of the danger." She paused. "But there was something else too."

"What?"

"I remember how he'd ask the same questions over the years about your health when you were a boy. I asked him more than once why he was so concerned, but he'd always just shrug it off. I couldn't figure it out."

"I know why he worried, Mom."

"You do?"

"Yes," I said. "There was something he didn't tell you about Herb."

CHAPTER 38

IT'S CLEAR TO ME NOW how very deep a relationship existed between your mother and our father," Herb observed as we sat together one night in the spring of 2001. We were at the small Italian restaurant near his apartment where we had begun to meet for dinner almost every week. "Your mother is giving me a whole new picture of my father—a picture I had never imagined. It's wonderful, Walter, because I never actually saw my father in a profound relationship with a woman."

"What about his relationship with your mother or his second wife, Janet?" I asked.

"Well," Herb replied, "my mother and father were separated for as long as I can remember. So I saw them together very little. I did, however, see him with Janet—but I saw no passion there. My father may have been content in the relationship with her, but I'm convinced now that it was nothing like what he and your mother had. And, as I've said before, the more I speak with your mother, the better I understand my father."

"Herb," I said, "you should know that my mother absolutely loves your calls . . ."

"And I like talking to *her*," he interrupted.

"She delights in talking to you about our father," I continued. "Every time I see her or speak to her on the telephone, she asks about you, and she always sends her love. She's enthralled with you, Herb. It's as if she's on a mission. She wants to tell you as much as she can while she still can."

"Walter," Herb stopped me. "What are you saying?"

"My mother is very ill," I replied.

Herb's eyes widened.

"She has chronic emphysema," I continued, "and heart and circulatory troubles. Herb, she's far sicker than she lets on to you."

"Should I keep calling?"

"Absolutely," I answered, but I explained that the doctors had her on prednisone and that she was worried about showing side effects of the drug, such as talking too much—silly chatter. "She wants to be alert for you," I said, "and if she can't . . ."

"She speaks perfectly well," Herb interrupted.

"You don't have to defend my mother to me!" I assured him.

I was about to continue when the waitress appeared with our food. We kibitzed good-naturedly with her until she finished. After she left, however, I grew serious again and said, "Herb, I told my mother that I knew something Al had kept from her, and it's something I learned from you."

"Really?" Herb asked. "What is that?"

"I told her I knew why Albert Dorfman was so worried about my health when I was a child."

HERBERT DORFMAN was born in 1928, a year before the stock market crash that plunged the United States into the Great Depression. He was four years old—an only child—when his parents separated. Soon after, so she could hold a full-time job, his mother shipped Herb from Brooklyn to the Bronx to live with a married couple she had found to care for him. The foster father was grouchy, though, and he greatly resented the small boy. It was a tense, unhappy household. Herb told me he learned to fend for himself, creating his own fantasies and adventures, making friends in the neighborhood—and avoiding, as much as possible, the man with whom he lived.

One afternoon his father—who had promised to bring Herb a toy, a small pinball machine—called on the telephone to say he couldn't make that day's planned visit. Hearing the news, Herb began to cry uncontrollably. Albert, hearing his son's sobs, picked up on the child's distress and changed his plans. Herb was euphoric when, only a short time later, he spotted his father walking down the block toward him, a large grin on his face and the pinball machine under his arm. Herb told me that he still remembers that afternoon as one of the most joyous of his childhood.

The visits to their son in the Bronx continued—sometimes his mother, sometimes his father, but the two rarely together.

As he neared seven, Herb felt increasingly ill—and it was apparent to his parents on their visits that their son was becoming progressively weaker. A medical examination at Lebanon Hospital in the Bronx was scheduled. The doctors told his parents that Herbert had been stricken with rheumatic fever, then reported an even more frightening discovery: the little boy had a puncture in his heart muscle.

Herbert subsequently was delivered to Irvington House, a residential treatment facility for children in Westchester County. There, he lived his days and nights tucked into a small bed or squeezed into a wheelchair. When he peered through a window in the building, he could see a dreamlike world of trees and roads and cars and colors and sounds, but none of it was available to him. He was too sick, he was told, to be allowed outside. The nurses and attendants—working among so many seriously ill children—were indifferent at best, impatient at worst. No one at Irvington House offered the boy a single gesture of affection or shared a funny story or kind word. He was like a broken toy, unwanted and discarded. His parents were allowed to visit for one hour once every six weeks, on a schedule approved by Irvington House. When his father occasionally missed a day, he didn't see his son for twelve weeks.

Herb told me that he ached with loneliness as the months dragged on ever so slowly. A year passed. Still, he remained.

One afternoon, he was wheeled into a large room lined with other children. He sat quietly as an attendant turned on a movie projector and *Captains Courageous* began. Gradually, Herb said, he found himself entranced with the fictional escapades of the young boy played by Freddie Bartholomew. *Freddie Bartholomew is the luckiest boy in the world*, Herb told himself, *and I am the unluckiest.*

Later, as the days and weeks continued to grind by, Herb reflected often on what he believed to be Freddie Bartholomew's good fortune—and slowly, at first almost imperceptibly, a steely resolve emerged from his festering anger: *I am going to get out of here,* he promised himself, *and I'll make my own fun.*

Trapped in an institution and surrounded by indifference, he confided his bitterness to no one and camouflaged his defiance behind a cloak of quiet stubbornness.

Finally, six months after his ninth birthday—and more than two years after he arrived at Irvington House—the doctors told his parents that the sickly boy had been rehabilitated: Herbert Dorfman, they declared, could go home.

Home? he wondered. *What home?*

Herb was sent to live with his father's relatives, where he remained for a year and a half—again in an unhappy household. Then, finally, his mother brought him to live with her in a single room rented in someone else's apartment in the Brighton Beach section of Brooklyn. Upon see-ing the place, Herb told me, he thought to himself, *Well, it's better than Irvington House.*

Over the next few years, Herb proved to be a good student, even becoming editor of his high school newspaper. After class, he worked variously as an usher in a local movie theater, a waiter, a busboy and a roofer laying tiles in the sun. *I'll earn my own way,* he pledged to him-self—and he kept his word.

Then, when he was seventeen, his parents finally divorced after years of separation.

Shortly thereafter, upon graduation from high school, Herb was offered a half-scholarship by New York University because of his aca-demic excellence. It was still more than he could afford, however, so he enrolled at Brooklyn College, where the tuition was considerably less.

He soon joined the college newspaper, the *Vanguard*, as a reporter and editor, working side by side with Mitchel Levitas, Myron Kandel, William Taylor and Rhoda Karpatkin—fellow students who would go on to become recognized leaders in communications or the law. Trouble arose for all of them, though, when the school's administration chal-lenged some of the articles in the *Vanguard*. When Herb and his col-leagues held firm, Brooklyn College revoked the newspaper's charter. The defiant students continued to publish off-campus.

Despite all these distractions, Herb continued to get good grades and completed Brooklyn College on time. But, he told me, he refused to attend graduation because of the school's action against the *Vanguard*. He subsequently enrolled in the graduate program at Columbia Uni-versity and earned a master of arts degree in political science in 1951.

By then, Herb told me, his urge to communicate had become irre-sistible. He was determined to write, and his resolve was unrelenting. He found a job as a reporter and an editor with the newspaper of the International Ladies Garment Workers Union and remained there a couple of years. Then Herb was awarded a Fulbright scholarship to study labor relations in Norway. He later wrote a book on the subject, published by the University of Wisconsin in 1956.

When Herb returned to New York City after the Fulbright experience, he quickly was hired by a local television station, where he flourished and eventually became a nationally recognized writer and producer of news and documentary television reports. And the name Herbert Dorfman was credited prominently nearly every night on the small screen, where it never failed to catch my mother's attention.

"WHAT DID SHE SAY when you told your mother about the problem with my heart when I was a child?" Herb asked.

"'*Aha*' was her exact word," I said. "And then she called Al a 'son of a gun' for not telling her about your heart. She thinks he didn't want to worry her unnecessarily, since she assured him that my health was OK whenever he asked. Incidentally, Loretta made me promise to get checked for a 'collagen disease,' since you told me our father died from that condition. I got checked, and I'm OK."

"That's good," said Herb. "By the way, was there anything else our father held back from your mother?"

"Yes," I replied. "He apparently shaved a couple of years off his age when he told her how old he was. That was worth another 'son of a gun.'"

Herb smiled. "Sometimes he'd also make up stories about me," he added. "I remember one time in particular when he told a guy—with me standing right there!—that I played basketball for Army. Can you imagine? I didn't even go to West Point. I asked him later why he said such a thing. He said the story he told would make me special to the other guy. I guess he felt a need to exaggerate. On the other hand, he was kind, never cruel, and could be very sensitive."

"That makes me wonder about something," I said.

"What's that?"

"To the best you can recollect," I asked, "did he ever come close to telling you about me? Or even hint?"

"I've certainly thought about it a lot," said Herb. "When his second wife did not get pregnant, he told me he was sure that *he* wasn't the problem. I asked how he could be so sure. He hesitated for a couple of seconds and then said that *I* was the proof—that *I* had been born. Looking back now, it's possible he came very close to telling me that day and then did not. My feeling is that he might have told me after your mother's husband had passed away, but he died first himself. Anyway, it's clear he kept their secret. And he never knew how truly similar we may have been.

"I mean," Herb continued, "it's astonishing when you think about it: two sons born sixteen years apart, both raised in dysfunctional homes, each living with difficulties you would wish on no child, neither one knowing of the other, both good students, both communicators."

I then confessed that, as we had shared more time together and I'd learned more about Herb's life, I had found the parallels in our careers and the similarities of our interests and abilities to be a little disconcerting. But then, ultimately, I found myself enjoying the fact that our lives had progressed in a like manner.

After a discussion of Albert Dorfman and our similarities, Herb changed the subject to William Anderson and my feelings of alienation. "Walter," he asked, "when did you know that you didn't belong, that you were different?"

"The truth is," I began, "I thought I was different from others in my family as early as I can remember. It wasn't so much how I looked but rather how I thought. It wasn't until I returned from Vietnam and had a confrontation with the man who raised me, however, that I knew he wasn't a blood relation. I can't explain it. It's just true: I *knew*. I guess I *always* knew, Herb. I just didn't know I knew. Still, when my mother confirmed the truth, it was shocking.

"And now I have a question for *you*," I continued. "Herb, what does it mean to you to be Jewish?"

"That's an interesting question," he replied, "because I haven't really been what you'd call an observant Jew."

He paused, reflecting.

"When I was young," Herb began, "I attended synagogue, but the truth is that I haven't done that in a long time. Yet I know I'm Jewish. But what does that mean? You know, even your friend Elie Wiesel would struggle with this. There's probably a better answer, but . . . well, I think partly it has to do with family . . . and then history . . . and tradition, of course. Let me see. I think there's a common feeling among Jews, an understanding—but what is it?"

I asked if it could be an understanding about *behavior*, and Herb agreed that behavior is central to being a Jew. He cited a responsibility toward other people, whether they are Jewish or not. "I've seen this in Jews around the world," said Herb. "It is . . . well, it is a sense of humanity . . . maybe of *consideration*. I know these are not the best words . . . but, Walter, I know I am a Jew."

"I understand," I said.

Herb then turned the tables again and asked what being Jewish meant to *me*. He said he knew that I'd been thinking about this for a very long time—since my mother first told me about Albert Dorfman.

"Like you," I began, "I would emphasize the importance of behavior. But I need to say this in my own way—because you're really asking me about *me*.

"Our father was Jewish," I continued, "but, because my mother was not Jewish, in the eyes of many people—especially other Jews—I cannot be Jewish."

"Is that important to you?" asked Herb.

"No," I replied. "I'm the only person who can answer for me."

"I agree," Herb said.

"But what I do lack, Herb, is something far more defining than an ancient decree about childbirth."

"Which is?"

"I have not *lived* as a Jew," I said. "And that is defining. Herb, I never knew our father. He never shared a single Jewish memory with me. Nevertheless, he was right when he told my mother that I was 'one Jewish boy who is not going to be hurt because he is a Jew.' I have been spared persecution and discrimination. However, what he didn't, or couldn't, acknowledge was what I would be *denied*. You have recollections, Herb. Even with the hard times you lived through, you remember Jewish family celebrations and observances like Yom Kippur and Hanukkah. They're a part of you. I remember Christmas trees."

I then told Herb that while I had read considerably about Judaism and could reasonably discuss the subject, when I *talked* about it, my experience was as an observer. "*Unless,*" I added, "I simply say what I feel and not necessarily what I can explain."

"Please do," he encouraged.

"When I was a boy," I said, "I chose not to be confirmed in a church. Was I, by my behavior, choosing to be 'chosen'? I don't know. What I *do* know is that the most rewarding moments of my life have been when I've struggled for something larger than myself." I mentioned, for example, that I found great fulfillment in tackling social problems such as illiteracy, racism and child abuse—and not just in the pages of *Parade*.

"Herb," I said, "the truth is that these tragedies are far more than just story topics for me to edit or to write about. I believe that each injustice we come upon is our personal responsibility to address, and when I don't respond to an inequity—or, worse, if I look the other way—I feel guilty."

"*Jewish* guilt?" he asked with a smile.

"Maybe," I said, returning his smile, "but there's a truth I can't ignore. Herb, I don't think that merely because our father was Jewish makes *me* Jewish. If I am Jewish, it is because my attitudes and behavior reflect a Jewish sensitivity."

"Walter," he asked, "do you *feel* Jewish?"

"That's the thing, Herb. I think I do."

CHAPTER 39

I T'S OK TO SAY GOODBYE NOW," I told my mother. It was July 8, 2001, and she was in a bed at White Plains Hospital, her body tethered by wires and intravenous devices.

It hurt not to cry, to keep my voice calm and to speak without inflection, but I knew a reassuring tone would make it easier for her. The emphysema had almost totally ravaged her lungs, and now her kidneys had failed. The circulation to her legs also had shut down—and the pain, despite a steady drip of drugs, was agonizing.

The duty nurse had advised me that my mother had, at most, hours left. "Mr. Anderson, your mother is hanging on by an act of will," she said. "You need to tell her it's all right to let go. You are the person she's most concerned about—and, believe me, you are the only one she will listen to."

"I love you, Mom," I said, and my voice cracked.

She smiled up from the hospital bed. "I am ready to die," she said slowly, struggling to be heard, her voice barely above a whisper. "Walter, I want to die."

"I know, Mom, and it's OK. You can let go."

Two hours later, with her granddaughter, Melinda, at the foot of her bed and her grandson, Eric, standing with me outside her door, she stopped breathing.

Melinda called out, "Daddy, you'd better come in."

The sound of the life-support systems continued unabated, whirring and hissing—all to no avail. The difference between life and death is stark, unmistakable. Her body had surrendered. I knew my mother was gone, even as I summoned her physician. In her place was a pale and cold reflection of who she had been. The doctor quickly confirmed the obvious.

It was as if the air were pulled from my body. I slumped forward and started to sob. Both of my children held me.

MY MOTHER'S BODY was laid out in an open casket, as she had requested, at the McMahon, Lyon & Hartnett Funeral Home in White Plains. Flower arrangements filled the room, their bouquet a fragrant mist.

Loretta and I were the first to arrive. As we drew closer to the coffin, I shuddered. Loretta squeezed my arm, but I pulled away. She quietly stepped back, understanding. Truly, I needed to be alone.

I knelt.

You gave me life, I thought, my eyes filling, a*nd you freed me with the truth. I'm going to miss you.*

I knew, of course, that my mother had been eighty-eight years old, in terrible pain, each breath a struggle. And I had understood for several weeks that she was about to die. Yet, as prepared as I thought I was— and recognizing indisputably that death was a blessing for my mother—I was, nonetheless, devastated.

"You can be made an orphan at any age, my friend," Elie Wiesel had told me, his voice consoling, soon after he heard about my mother's death.

Elie understands, Mom. This hurts more than I ever expected.

I looked at her face. The morticians, working their craft from the pictures Loretta and I had given them, had honored their art.

"They made her look so beautiful," Loretta said softly.

A FEW WEEKS EARLIER, after several emergency visits to White Plains Hospital and a stay at a rehabilitation facility, my mother had carefully selected the white blouse and black slacks she wanted to wear for her burial. She neatly hung the garments in her closet, pinned with a note of instructions for Loretta, all of which had been carried out to the last detail.

"Where do you think you're going?" I asked my mother at the time.

"Very soon I'm going to be seeing everybody who's gone, honey. There's no medical magic left for me. And, to tell you the truth, I'm pretty tired, and everything hurts."

My mother then asked me to remember to go through her belongings in her apartment with care after she died. When I did, I found notes she had secreted like Easter eggs, all meant to be discovered. Most were written in prose, some in rhyme. She thanked Loretta several times for the care my wife had given her during the last few years. My mother described repeatedly how much she appreciated her family. In one note, she reminded me twice to tell Herb Dorfman how pleased she was that she had lived to meet him.

Her messages had given me an idea: I held aside one letter to give to my son, who I knew would deliver the eulogy on behalf of our family at his grandmother's funeral.

And now the funeral parlor was filling quickly.

I felt a hand on my shoulder. I turned, and there was my brother Herb. "I'll miss her too," he said softly.

"My grandmother *LOVED*," Eric began, "and she loved with enthusiasm. I was honored that she and Grandpa in their final years shared a home with Claudia, Jonathan and me. So much of Grandma spans the generations. She loved to read and to write, for example. Is it such a surprise, then, that my father and my sister are writers, and all of us in this family are avid readers? Her great love of cooking is shared by me, my sister and, of course, my mother. And her love of travel—well, count how many countries that my sister, Melinda, alone has visited. How about Grandma's energy? She competed in dance contests until she was in her mid-seventies—and she won! She wrote songs and she wrote poetry. And she encouraged every one of us to be a risk-taker.

"So today we recognize that we, the Andersons, are her legacy. But wait! Why should I struggle for words when I know that hers would be more appropriate? Let me share with you some of my grandmother's own words. Listen to her voice, from a letter she wrote to my dad. In truth, I think you'll agree, it's a message for all of us:

> *Even when I am no longer here on earth, I live within you . . . I will always be a part of you . . . A mother's love does not have to die . . . It can live on in her children . . . I have often thought of how a mother has her children within her for nine months. Yes, they are hers alone for a while. Then, though, they are born, and their love is shared. Life is so wonderful. Death must be known by rich and poor alike. We shed a tear when someone we love dies, but the living go on. No regrets. God bless you all.*

"Imagine, at eighty-eight, being able to say 'no regrets.' What a wonderful way to say goodbye. Goodbye, Grandma."

A FEW WEEKS LATER, my mother's younger sister, Florence Thiele, told me: "Your mother would have been so pleased with how they made up her face so beautifully. And now she'll be beautiful forever."

Yes, she will.

AUTHOR'S NOTE

It was early in the morning of April 3, 2001. I was seated in a crowded, bustling waiting area in New York's LaGuardia Airport, not far from the gate I'd be passing through for a flight to Denver. I was reading the day's edition of the *New York Times* when I happened to glance up and recognize another passenger.

"Elie!" I called out.

"Walter, my friend, how *are* you?" Elie Wiesel replied, and when I stood, we embraced.

Once aboard the flight, I asked whether we could move so that Elie and I might be seated next to each other. A helpful flight attendant made the change easily.

As the plane lifted from the ground, I began, "I have some news . . ."

Elie listened intently, nodding slowly as I spoke, encouraging me. I told him all that I had learned so far about my real father and the Dorfman family, their Russian history, and I described the unexpected warmth I felt toward Herbert, whom I had only recently met.

When I finished speaking, we both sat quietly—and then Elie spoke: "You must write this story."

A great deal of effort far beyond my own goes into a book like this, to be sure, and there are a number of persons I wish to thank: Elie Wiesel and his wife, Marion, dear friends who steadfastly encouraged me through some of the most sensitive parts of this story and who were, in fact, the first to read the original manuscript of *Meant To Be*; my wife, Loretta, whose compassion for my mother, especially in my mother's last few months, was heroic and unforgettable; our son, Eric, the thoughtful, sensitive man whose curiosity eventually led to our family's first meeting with the Dorfmans; our daughter, Melinda, who put aside some of her own work as an author and as an editor to help me do the required research and reporting (and who, without hesitation, edited her father); our daughter-in-law, Claudia, a third-grade teacher in the Bronx, who all in our family call *our* Mrs. Williams; Ilza Williams herself, who passed away while I was still writing this story, but whose legacy continues to live in the lives she touched, my own included; my lifelong friend, the incredibly gifted Barry Williams, of whom his mother was so proud—and whom she kept in line; my niece, Robin Farrow, whose generosity of spirit, whose love and thoughtfulness, made all the difference; Esther Dorfman, who enthusiastically supported me throughout this adventure; the distinguished reporter Bernard Gavzer, whose will, skill and courage make the very difficult look so easy.

Again, a book is ultimately a collaborative work and it was never truer than with *Meant To Be*. Jane Friedman, the supportive CEO of Harper-Collins, has been steadfast in her enthusiasm. Martin Timins of *Parade* adroitly copy-edited the original manuscript before I turned it over to my highly talented editor at HarperCollins, Gail Winston. (What Gail described to me at first, ever so innocently, as "minor" questions invariably seemed to lead to major revisions—but every suggestion she made, I'm happy to report, markedly improved the book.) I'd also like to thank Christine Walsh of HarperCollins for her help and Roberto de Vicq de Cumptich and Chin-Yee Lai, who designed the cover. I am grateful to my assistant, AnneMarie Palmer, and to all of my colleagues at *Parade*. Lee Kravitz, Isadore Rosenfeld, Steve Newhouse, Maurie Perl and Larry Smith went out of their way to give me solid advice as did my pal Jerry Lewis, who, as always, helped me smile through some of the tough spots.

Throughout the publishing process of *Meant To Be* I have been guided by the brilliant and sensitive Sandi Mendelson, who is deservedly one of the most successful public relations executives in the country.

Each writer should be fortunate enough to have an agent like Jack Scovil, unfailingly patient and wise . . . and therein lies a story. Because I was so sensitive to the content of my story and the lives involved— questioning myself whether, in fact, I should even write a book—Jack decided to introduce me to Cathy Hemming, the president and publisher of HarperCollins. I was anxious. It was the first time I would share with anyone outside of a very small circle the truth of my birth. Cathy responded warmly, though, and with a rare understanding. Later, as Jack and I walked down Lexington Avenue in Manhattan, we were certain we had found the right publisher. And we were right. Thank you, Cathy.

Finally, there are two whose contributions to *Meant To Be* were largest of all: My mother, of course, and Herbert Dorfman, whose candor, wisdom and trust made so much of this story worth telling.

Herb and I talk frequently now. My life is better with him in it. I seem to learn something almost every time we speak. Well, that's no surprise. He is, after all, my brother.

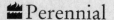 Perennial

Books by Walter Anderson:

MEANT TO BE
The True Story of a Son Who Discovers He Is His Mother's Deepest Secret
ISBN 0-06-009907-0 (paperback)

Anderson, a 21-year-old Marine, returns from service to say good-bye to his dying father and tries to find the answer to a question that has inexplicably haunted him from his earliest years: Was the alcoholic, abusive man who so tormented him in his childhood his real father? Shockingly, the answer turns out to be "No." His mother, a German Protestant, fell in love during World War II with a Russian Jew and bore his child. Although Anderson learns this as a young man, he and his mother keep this secret for another 35 years, until the day Anderson meets an unknown brother living a nearly parallel life.

"I have rarely read in recent years a narrative written with such intensity, emotion, and elegance. I warmly recommend it to all readers, whatever their faith."
—Elie Wiesel

THE CONFIDENCE COURSE
Seven Steps to Self-Fulfillment
ISBN 0-06-109453-6 (paperback) • ISBN 0-694-51782-8 (audio)

An inspiring step-by-step guide to overcoming self-doubt and achieving personal and professional success based on Anderson's popular course at the New School for Social Research in New York City. Anderson teaches you how to choose what you want to be. In 20 interactive lessons, complete with exercises and real-life examples, Anderson offers rules to live by that can positively transform your life.

"Clear, concise, and inspiring. An easy, interesting, and fast read, filled with meaty material for the mind and heart—the three-plus pages about giving and taking criticism alone are worth the price." —Dan Rather